FINANCIAL PLANNING FOR THE **99%**

FINANCIAL PLANNING

for the 99%

FINANCIAL PLANNING FOR THOSE WHO NEED IT MOST

"Steps a person living with low to moderate income can take to invest better, reduce their income taxes, and spend better. Financial planning in terms that everyone can understand".

Wilbert Guilford, Jr, CFP®, CPA

MILL CITY PRESS

Mill City Press, Inc.
2301 Lucien Way #415
Maitland, FL 32751
407.339.4217
www.millcitypress.net

Paperback ISBN-13: 978-1-6628-6257-1
Hard Cover ISBN-13: 978-1-6628-6258-8
Ebook ISBN-13: 978-1-6628-6259-5

MY GOAL
TO TELL THE TRUTH AND TO MAKE A DIFFERENCE

"If like me you are intimidated by financial books, Guilford offers an easy guide to financial planning. You will understand how taxes and inflation affect your savings and learn to improve your finances, no matter your age or experience. This book is packed with information and options for life insurance, long term care insurance, and Medicare. You'll see how to build an investment portfolio and manage debt and credit. Wilbert has created an informative financial toolkit."

—*Blaise Lantana, Music Director, and Jazz Host.*

"Nice Style, easy to read. Wil's love of teaching shine's through."

—*Frank Crump, Founder/President, UPI Loan Fund.*

"This book is written in a clear concise manner, easily understood by all—no matter your financial background. Having a knowledge of financial options and plans is vital to living a life free of stress and loss for those who need financial guidance the most. The book is written in layman's language to ensure understanding and comprehension. We are fortunate Wilbert spent the past seven years of his life putting together much needed financial advice. I recommend this book for everyone".

—*JoAnn Blue, R.N., M.S.N., Adjunct Nursing Clinical Educator.*

"We have been using Mr. Guilford's financial services for nearly three decades. We rate him a five star ★★★★★ plus"

—*Reverend James & Mrs. Gail Griffin.*

Preface

The inspiration for this book grew from my desire to help people living with low and moderate income, but it will be helpful to those with higher incomes as well. This comprehensive book covers more than twenty-five important areas of finance. It includes intelligent investing, managing debt and credit, reducing income taxes, retirement planning, and a whole lot more. I was concerned that the financial services industry was not addressing the needs of most Americans and that 99 percent of Americans did not use a financial advisor! Since I began my life's journey about 75 years ago, I have seen and experienced a great number of financial transactions.

Growing up in a housing project in New Orleans, I learned about struggle at an early age. In the early 1960s my father earned $50 a week and my mother earned $35, about $340 a month. And yet my two sisters and I led full, productive, and enjoyable lives. With hundreds of kids of all ages, abilities, and ambitions to play with and shape my personality, I would not change that experience for anything in the world. In case you are wondering, $340 a month would equal about $1,800 a month in today's dollars. For various reasons it would be difficult for a family of five to live on that today.

After four years of active duty Air Force, I returned home and attended Loyola University and graduated with a BA in accounting in 1979. I then found a position as an auditor with the State of Connecticut, attended the University of Hartford, and completed a graduate degree in accounting in 1984. After graduation I accepted a position as an auditor with the Department of Defense and became a Certified Public Accountant in 1987.

As a CPA, I performed audit, tax, and accounting services for governmental agencies and businesses of all shapes and sizes. A significant part of my career included roles as a Facilitator and Leadership and Management Instructor in the Air Force Reserves. I also taught accounting as an Adjunct Professor at Southern University in New Orleans.

By the year 2000, many clients had begun asking questions about investing, life insurance, and saving for retirement. I knew financial planners and insurance agents were better equipped to answer those questions. So I began a quest to become a Certified Financial Planner™ and licensed insurance agent. I accomplished both in 2004.

As a CFP® I looked forward to hanging out my shingle and providing financial advice to the people who first inspired me to study financial planning. But that would not be as easy as you might think. I wanted to get some experience and the financial services industry charged a high price for admission. And I don't just mean in dollars.

Shortly after becoming a CFP®, I landed a position with a major financial services firm. There I learned of the industry's practice of selling investments while paying advisors on commission. Providing financial advice was simply incidental to sales transactions. Meeting sales quotas was more important than helping certain communities or people with particular financial challenges. Neither my firm nor others in the industry seemed interested in tapping into the market of millions of Americans living with low and moderate income. Actually my firm was considered more humanitarian than most others, but the priority of meeting sales quotas still outweighed all other considerations.

The pressure to sell investments pushed many advisors to engage in unethical behavior, even fraud. But as a CPA and member of the military, I had become accustomed to following the highest of standards in my work. When someone's life or financial well-being depends upon whether or not you exercise integrity, you tend to take your work seriously. And I could not reconcile working without a dependable salary while being restricted from the part-time work I needed and wanted to pursue. So I resigned from the financial services firm and went back to performing accounting work. I retired as an auditor from the State of Arizona in 2015.

Though I left the financial services firm in 2005, I continued to provide tax and financial advice part-time. Since 2015 I have provided financial counseling to members of the military stateside and overseas. This book is a compilation of my tax and financial planning knowledge and experience. I believe my audit and accounting skills add great breadth and depth to the book. My perspective on the financial services industry is likely shaped by my auditing and military experience .

I won't pretend to know the perfect model for compensating advisors and pricing financial services. But the financial service industry's unpopularity and lack of diversity is probably a result of its current compensation and pricing practices. A survey by the business television network CNBC (in November 2019) found that 99 *percent* of Americans do not use a financial advisor (1). Only 18 percent of financial advisors are women and only 4 percent of financial advisors are Black or Hispanic (2).

But in a time when companies don't seem to value employees as much as they used to, most of us could benefit from expert financial advice. In efforts to maximize stock prices, companies have cut back on employee benefits. Most American workers must now rely on 401ks and IRAs for their retirement income. And companies now are more likely to hire independent contractors than full-time employees.

As inflation in 2021 and 2022 has shown, our dollar is continually at risk of losing it's purchasing power. Because wage increases and cost of living increases in social security and other benefits have not kept up with inflation, proper investing is crucial for folks living with low or moderate income.

But there are always some bright spots in the American economy for it is the largest in the world. Even so, with the many financial challenges we face, it is a must to make the most of every resource available to us. We have to play a significant role in our financial planning because most Americans are not included in the market financial advisors will likely pursue to be successful.

After providing accounting, tax, and financial planning advice for more than four decades, I was inspired to share that knowledge and experience. I have helped people from all walks of life and most income brackets. Because of the many significant financial topics covered, I am confident the book will be helpful to most who read it, about 99%.

Sincerely,

Wilbert E Guilford, Jr. LLC

January 2, 2023

In Memory Of:

David Graeber, the anthropologist, organizer of the Occupy Wall Street Movement and coiner of the phrase, "We are the 99%," and the author of *Debt, the First 5,000 years* (1961–2020).

A special acknowledgement to my family and friends, who helped me and love me, in spite of my failings.

Website: https://guilfordtaxman.com/
Email: wgcpa@q.com or guilfordw@gmail.com/

Introduction

I f you ever want to learn something, write a book about it. You will spend so much time trying to make sure your words are correct; you will learn much of what you didn't know before. This book includes a lot of what I learned after I started this book seven years ago.

This book will show you how to create an ideal portfolio of investments and avoid paying commissions (that can be five percent of your investment in most cases). You will learn how to efficiently reduce debts and improve your credit score. The book includes in-depth discussions and strategies to take advantage of tax credits and tax deductions. It even analyzes cryptocurrency, stripping away its mystery, providing perspective, and talking about it in terms the average person can understand.

The book will be helpful to people of all ages and income brackets. It uses illustrations, worksheets, webpage links, and detailed steps for better understanding of financial strategies and concepts. Life insurance, annuities, reverse mortgages, and long-term care are analyzed in detail. The book discusses the practices of the financial services industry and elaborates on U.S. tax policies over the past 50 years.

You will learn the substance of Medicare Supplement Plans and Medicare Advantage plans (like those advertised on TV). The advantages and disadvantages of taking social security at different ages are explored. The book covers student loan repayment options, basics of business development, and the home purchase process. Strategies for buying and leasing cars are discussed. Estate planning is included with suggestions to transfer property to your heirs. The financial services industry's compensation and pricing practices favor those with higher incomes. This book fills the void created by those practices.

In President Biden's joint address to Congress on April 28, 2021, he stated, "Six hundred and fifty billionaires (650) increased their wealth by more than one trillion dollars during this pandemic and they're now worth more than four trillion dollars." (He was speaking of the year 2020). Four trillion dollars is more than the entire federal budget of the United States (3.7 trillion dollars). So the wealthy have done well even in the worst of times. But if you are living with low or moderate income, what can you do to increase your wealth?

There are three things we can do to increase our wealth: spend better, reduce our taxes, and invest better. This book will show you how to do all three.

Knowledge of finance can bring us prosperity and comfort. On the other hand, the lack of financial knowledge can be a source of stress and loss—often for those who need financial guidance the most. Efforts to address financial education in the United States have been lackluster. It has sparingly been taught in America's senior high schools. Even for college business majors, Personal Finance is an elective course, if offered at all. The Consumer Financial Protection Bureau (CFPB) has made efforts to educate and protect the public since it began operations in 2011. But financial education in the United States has been underfunded and unorganized, leaving most people to fend for themselves.

This book provides a comprehensive education on personal finance. Layman's language is used throughout to provide understanding and perspective. A glossary is provided for explanation and reference.

To successfully plan financial activities, you should first establish clear goals for yourself and your family. But financial planning will be more challenging when you have multiple, competing goals. You will then have to prioritize. You will need to determine which resources to apply to which goals and when. After you decide upon strategies to accomplish your goals, you will create a plan. The final step is to implement the plan. Adding to our challenges are the number of people trying to sell us goods and services (that *they* say will help us meet all of our needs)!

Accompanying the salesperson is the psychology of getting us to pay more for things than we should. One good tool I've found helpful when dealing with aggressive salespeople is living by a spending plan (or budget). A spending plan is a numerical picture, a snapshot of what is important to us. It reflects what *you* value. If a potential purchase does not fit into your spending plan, refuse to make the purchase. Say no!

There are telltale signs when a deal is not good for you. (1) Your gut tells you it is a bit pricy while the salesperson is saying it is a substantial bargain! (2) There is pressure to close the deal ASAP. (3) The salesperson will move mountains to assist you to close the deal. And (4) The salesperson has solicited an emotional response from you. (i.e. they told a sad story about a family member or an event that weighed on your sympathies).

Even if the story they told is true, a stranger should not play on your emotions when engaging in an arms-length business transaction. If you saw another person experiencing the same circumstances you would probably tell them not to do a deal. So you will need to dig deep within yourself and say no. I have a spending plan template you might find helpful at my website: https://guilfordtaxman.com/ Click on the Services tab under Budgeting.

Your spending plan should be developed before you start detailed financial planning. That will help you visualize where you are financially and help you consider what's possible. After you have established goals and developed a financial plan, you will need to revise the budget. The budget or spending plan may need to be revised frequently. The spending plan is a most important tool in the financial planning process.

Many elements of a financial plan may require some knowledge of other elements. Retirement planning requires knowledge of investing. Investing requires knowledge of income taxes. Income taxes should also be considered in your choices for college savings, life insurance, or even the form of business you select (like a corporation, LLC, sole proprietor, or partnership).

Because these elements are interconnected, it's a good idea to consider tactics for each one (investments, insurance, payments on debts, etc.) But hold off on implementing the tactic until you have a tactic for each element and an overall strategy and plan. In other words, you want to create a final plan that will *optimize* your *total* earnings and *total* savings. That said, reducing income taxes alone can go a long way towards achieving many goals. Good tax management can increase your current income *and* savings over your lifetime that help build your nest egg.

With a Traditional IRA, you can get a tax deduction now and defer (postpone) income taxes until retirement. Or if you chose a Roth IRA, you wouldn't get a tax deduction now, but you could have *tax-free* income in future years. A good strategy is to have both a Roth IRA and a Traditional IRA in place each year (assuming you qualify for both). Just remember not to contribute more than the maximum contributions allowed in any one year. You can't double-dip. You can't duplicate the maximum contribution to both types of IRAs! The traditional IRA has a lower adjusted gross income threshold (so if your income in a particular year is higher, you may only qualify to contribute to a Roth IRA.

A third type of useful account is the brokerage, individual, or so-called non-retirement account. You will want to have this type of account open so when the stock market is down (as in the Spring and Summer of 2022) you can buy stocks or stock mutual funds at discounted prices. Then you can participate in the growth of the stock market without having to leave your investments in until age 59 & ½ as you do with 401Ks, deferred compensation plans, and IRAs (the retirement accounts).

The Traditional IRA can be helpful in more than one way. A person with low or moderate income can reduce his or her taxable income during working years. Then during retirement, they can use the standard deduction and personal exemptions to reduce their taxable income as they take withdrawals from the accounts! That's the definition of win/win. Creating tax-saving strategies is much better than the tax evasion tactics that get many people into trouble with the IRS.

Even when you receive earnings in cash (*the underground economy*), you can benefit from reporting the income on tax returns. After taking legitimate tax credits, allowable deductions, and making Traditional IRA contributions, your tax liabilities could be far less than you think. Plus your IRA investment will be in place to grow and enrich your life in your retirement. But you have to file your tax returns by April 15th to take advantage of IRA deductions. There is even a Qualified Business Income Deduction (QBI) just for having a profitable business (The QBI is expected to expire after 2025, unless extended).

Another significant benefit of filing tax returns is building up your credits to be eligible for social security. Social security provides a retirement income benefit for your lifetime *and* lifetime Medicare health coverage. For many people, social security income may account for a significant part of their retirement income. But you *must* accumulate a minimum of forty credits from working to qualify. Four credits can be earned per year, for at least ten working years (they don't have to be consecutive years). Income from self-employment also qualifies for the credits. If you become disabled, you could draw benefits sooner than your full *social security* retirement age. Reporting your taxable income can help you achieve financial independence in other ways too.

When you want to buy a home, get a home equity loan, or buy a car, the bank (or credit union) will ask for copies of your last three tax returns. Expect inquiries on the status of your tax returns if you need a security clearance for employment or when you apply for a professional license. So there is much more to gain by complying with the tax laws than by hiding in the shadows. You should hire a good tax professional to help file your tax returns. Credit is another area of finance we must be careful with.

Credit can help us achieve important goals like buying a home, car, or funding education. It can even play a role in a business venture. But credit can become a burden if we are not careful. You'll find chapters in the book on good credit management and paying back debt.

A major area of life and finance that we do not give enough thought to is retirement. Maybe we underestimate how challenging it will be or we overestimate our ability to prepare for it. The book provides detailed instructions enabling *you* to calculate how much you will need to save monthly for the retirement income you would like (stated in terms of present and future values of dollars).

Trying to build a nest egg for retirement has been compared to trying to fill a piggy bank that has small holes at the bottom. Three holes that come to mind are: taxes, interest, and inflation. Separately they may not trouble us, but together they can greatly impact our efforts to become financially independent. Inflation was the sneaky one until it reared its ugly head in 2021.

A dollar today is worth only 13 percent of what it was in 1967. Back then, a soft drink and bag of potato chips cost only ten cents (five cents each). A bus ride was only ten cents, and a plate of beans was only thirty-five cents (rice and smoked sausage were included). Inflation and age are not close relatives, but they are related. They are usually gradual, and we don't like to pay attention to either of them. And in some years, we take better care of ourselves than others.

To illustrate the effect of inflation and taxes, suppose you invested $10,000 in bonds, and the bonds earned 5 percent interest annually. The investment would have grown to $12,763 in five years. If your combined federal and state income tax rates were 25 percent, your taxes would be $691 (25 percent times $2,763). You now have left $12,072 ($12,763 less $691). If inflation during the five years were 3 percent (annually), you would need to subtract another $1,374 to reflect your loss of purchasing power. You can now purchase only $10,698 in goods or services ($12,072 less $1,374).

Investing the $10,000 into a conservative investment was a good move, but inflation had twice the negative effect on your purchasing power as the taxes! If you wanted to buy more than an additional $698 of goods and services after tying up your money for five years, you needed to have invested more aggressively (perhaps with stocks). But it's risky to invest in stocks if you have only a five-year time horizon. Investing in stocks will help us beat inflation but that requires that we have time and we start investing sooner. The last challenge, interest expense, can be just as sneaky as inflation.

If you are paying interest on debts, you need to deal with that hole in the bottom of the piggy bank too. You may find at times you can't decide on which positive goal to address—invest in more stocks, add to your savings account, or buy bonds for safety? That would be a perfect time to set a (low) dollar limit on your credit card balances or other interest charging accounts (that is if you can't pay them off completely every month).

To illustrate, let's say you have a goal of earning an average of 9% on your investments and savings. That will require strategy on your part. But if you are paying 11% interest on a credit card, that interest expense is baked in, and you are 2 percentage points behind even if you are successful at achieving 9% on your investments.

Credit used to buy a home or car is a good use of credit. Even with those purchases you will want to get the lowest interest rates you can negotiate. There may even be a chance to get a tax deduction for interest you pay on a home or car, but most other interest is just a drain on your efforts to achieve other financial goals. The book will show you effective ways to deal with debt as well as credit.

Financial planning is a lot like playing a football game. You need to use strategy, principles of finance, and the laws of probability to your advantage. It's great to have good players (assets and time on your side). But how you play offense or defense at any point in the game should be based on the laws of probability and the strengths of your assets (strong front line, nifty running back, or fast wide receiver). Even with your strengths in place, if you do not use the principles of finance and the laws of probability to your advantage, you could lose the game. And in the game of life, we may not have the same good players on our team the next time the opportunity to play comes around.

The comments above are just a sample of the financial concepts and ideas covered in the book. The book includes thoughtful strategies for making and saving money, explained in simple terms. Financial planning is not as critical as our health, but in a world where money is so important, we have to give money the attention it deserves.

Table of Contents

1. The Financial Services Industry................................ 1
2. The Financial Planning Process............................... 8
3. Spending Plans (Budgeting)................................. 10
4. Financial Goal Setting and Strategies....................... 15
5. Income Tax Saving Strategies 18
6. Insurance (Sharing Risks, What Kind and How Much?) 31
7. Long Term Care (LTC) Insurance 39
8. Investing: The Road to a Better Future 52
9. Home Buying 83
10. Car Buying 88
11. Retirement Planning (Your Transition to a Better Lifestyle) 94
12. Education 108
13. Annuities.. 113
14. Health Savings Accounts 119
15. Medicare, Medicare Advantage, & Medigap Plans............ 121
16. When to Draw Social Security 126
17. Reverse Robin Hood and the Taxman 130
18. How to Organize a Business:............................. 137
19. Where to Shop and Invest 143
20. Managing Credit 149

21. Effective Ways to Reduce Debt 152

22. Paying Back Student Loans 155

23. Offers in Compromise..................................... 159

24. Reverse Mortgages (Pros and Cons) 161

25. Estate Planning (Survivorship Planning, Avoiding Probate).... 164

26. Cryptocurrency 170

27. Afterword 180

Bibliography 183

Glossary.. 187

Financial Planning for the 99 Percent

Financial Planning for Those Who Need It Most

The United States provides a great nesting box for incubating some of the world's most successful businesses. Consider that Microsoft, Apple, Google, Amazon, and a multitude of tech companies were born right here in the US. But our capitalistic experiment does have its imperfections. I wish everyone were paid based upon their effort, their abilities, and the value of their contributions to society. But we know that many people are not paid all they are worth. And powerful interests to this day limit opportunities for deserving people.

When the Constitution was written, only men with property were allowed to vote. Although we now have the ability to vote, billions of dollars are spent telling us for *whom* to vote, then additional billions are spent telling elected officials for *what* to vote. Most of that money is spent to achieve private or corporate goals, not goals that contribute to the public good or the prosperity of the working class. Even as this book is being written, privileged interests are attempting to pass state laws allowing *independent* state legislatures to set aside the majority vote so the state legislature would decide who will be President or Senator. The Supreme Court will soon decide whether states will be allowed to do that! I can't make the world more democratic, but I hope to provide you some opportunities for leveling the financial playing field.

My goal with this book is to help you become financially independent. I think we can agree that the fewer people in financial need, the better society will be for us all. Unfortunately, a few powerful people are convinced that manipulating our economic system to their advantage is simply good business. And I suppose many in the financial professions have played a role in that thinking, believing their prosperity depended primarily on helping those with significant means acquire more means. But who provides financial guidance to the majority of Americans who are simply trying to make ends meet or improve *their* standard of living? Not enough help has been provided to those who rely on their labor to improve their lot in life.

One industry that could play a major role in improving the lot of more Americans is the financial services industry.

CHAPTER 1
The Financial Services Industry

The financial services industry can work well for those with substantial means. The activities of financial advisors are regulated at both the federal and state levels. The Securities and Exchange Commission (SEC) requires public companies undergo strict financial audits resulting in the trust of investors around the world. But the fact that only a small percentage of Americans use financial advisors is an indication of problems in the financial services industry.

The financial service industry's business models of selling investments and managing fortunes have not addressed the need for financial advice of the majority of Americans. Selling investments is so important to the industry that even people from other professions are allowed into the ranks of advisors if they display the potential to sell. As a result of commission sales and other industry practices, the financial services industry suffers from widespread fraud, lack of diversity, and lack of appreciation by the majority of Americans.

A major consequence of Industry practices and government regulations is less availability of financial advice for those living with low and moderate incomes. Complex and cumbersome government regulations provide big banks and Wall Street firms with market advantages while they dissuade finance and accounting professionals from providing financial advice directly to the public.

The commission pay practices of the financial services industry may be the primary reason financial advice is not provided to more people. Simply put, a 5% commission on the sale of a $100,000 investment will give an advisor ten times the paycheck of 5% on a $10,000 sale. Furthermore, most, if not all financial service firms require a substantial investment to manage a portfolio of investments for you. In fact, many financial firms expect candidates for employment to bring aboard with them clients and money they expect to manage as an employee of the firm!

An additional concern are industry regulations that permit employers to hire and license financial advisors who have little or no formal financial education. That practice limits opportunities for those with formal finance and accounting education. Those non-financial professionals are hired because of their potential to sell. Industry regulations allow anyone passing a couple of securities exams and with limited experience to sell investment products. Selling products has become more important to the industry than providing financial guidance to the public at large.

I could be wrong, I often am, but selling skills has nothing to do with one's ability to provide good financial advice. If they did, sales would be taught in one of the many finance and accounting courses required to earn a degree in finance or accounting. But as a manager from a major broker/ dealer firm (who was also a CPA) said to me, "I would rather teach a used car salesman finance than teach a CPA to sell. The CPA will be trying to make sure his calculations are correct, while the used car salesman knows when to close!" Note to reader: It's a good thing for the person providing you financial advice to double check their figures. But the commission sales practice is only one of many questionable industry policies.

Another reason financial advice may not be provided to more people is that employers place the cost of operations and marketing expenses on the backs of financial advisors. Employers routinely charge advisors for the use of proprietary company computers, sales materials, supplies, and more. Advisors are also responsible for travel expenses, which can be significant in a sales-oriented environment. Thus financial advisors do not have the time or financial interest to help people living with low or moderate incomes.

If the commission pay policies and cost of operations are not burden enough for financial advisors, industry employers can even prevent advisors from pursuing part-time work of their choosing. Of course part-time work might not be necessary if advisors received a dependable base salary to begin with! But complicated financial industry regulations push many accounting, finance, and business school graduates to work for the big banks and Wall Street firms that engage in the practices mentioned above.

The way the industry operates, an advisor who majored in Foreign Films and had wealthy contacts would be more likely to succeed than someone with an MBA or finance degree from the same university (who had fewer wealthy contacts). Potential clients with low or moderate income are left out of the picture altogether. Any number of financial advisors would get in line to help someone manage significant wealth. They will even offer discounts to manage wealth in excess of one million dollars. But there is just no incentive or motivation to assist someone living on a limited budget, who might only be able to purchase a small investment. Providing financial advice is only a biproduct of the sales transaction.

The emphasis on selling investment products results in a tremendous amount of corrupt advisor behavior. The *Financial Advisor IQ* newsletter reports daily on findings of fictitious sales, forgery, wire fraud, churning, and embezzlement (3). In 2020, an advisor was even charged with murdering a client (4). In August 2021, *Financial Advisor IQ* reported that a financial advisor was going to prison for stealing $800,000 from a client (5). The client had received his money as a settlement after being falsely imprisoned. That's called adding insult to injury!

On November 5, 2021, *Financial Advisor IQ* reported the following quote from the Chair of the Securities and Exchange Commission (SEC), Gary Gensler, "Unfortunately, I've learned in my first six months that there are too many fraudsters, penny stock scammers, Ponzi scheme architects, and pump-and-dump cons taking advantage of investors." "Think of a football game," Gensler continued. "Teams, without fear of penalties, start to break the rules. The game isn't fair, and maybe after a few minutes, it isn't fun to watch. Without examination against and enforcement of our rules and laws, we can't instill the trust necessary for our markets to thrive" (6).

With both an audit and financial background, my perspective on the financial services industry might be more critical than others. For experienced auditors know that *stress, rationalization, and opportunity* are *the* three conditions that lead to fraud. Stress is caused from lack of a dependable salary. Paying for operational expenses without a basic salary or freedom to work part-time can lead to rationalization (I am being taken advantage of). All that's needed then is opportunity. And opportunities seem to be found every day! The same seeds that move the advisor to commit fraud can also give rise to another vice—materialism.

In September 2011, the Occupy Wall Street Movement exposed the greed of Wall Street executives along with economic disparities in the United States. As millions of Americans lost their homes and jobs, Wall Street executives took home multi-million-dollar bonuses and none of that greed violated financial industry regulations.

Wall Street firms and large banks negotiate with financial industry regulators on the rules they will follow. Together, they make providing financial services to the public unnecessarily cumbersome and complicated. Large banks and Wall Street firms have whole departments dedicated to deal with convoluted and confusing regulations. Regulators simply referee a game in which the winners and losers have already been chosen.

The distinguished economist Robert Reich wrote about influencers of government policies in his book, *Saving Capitalism*, "This is not corruption as commonly understood (he says). In the United States, those with power and resources rarely directly bribe public officials . . . Instead they make campaign contributions and occasionally hold out the promise of lucrative jobs . . . And the most valuable things they get in exchange are *market rules that seems to apply to everyone and appear to be neutral*, but that systematically and disproportionately benefit them" (7).

In ethics training we often hear integrity defined as 'doing what's right even when no one is looking'. But I find it is even harder to do what's right if it means going against the crowd while *everyone* is looking. I went against the crowd because the financial needs of the people I became a financial advisor to help were not being addressed. If one didn't have much money, they were ignored (or quickly sold something that would not improve their situation or might even make it worse!) As Howard Zinn used to say to his students, "You can't be neutral on a moving train."

Maybe the industry's lack of diversity explains why such unfair practices continue. Or maybe the unfair practices explain why there is such a lack of diversity? The culture and policies of the industry were designed to comply with SEC Regulations from the 1930s and the Investment Advisors Act of 1940. Back then few women or minorities had a voice in government or business.

Today only 18 percent of financial advisors are women. Only 4 *percent* of financial advisors are Black or Hispanic (2). Consider the following comments caught on video in August 2021 from a TikTok post of a CEO of a financial advisory firm in Texas. She was complaining after interviewing a Black job applicant. "I specifically said no Blacks. I'm not prejudiced, but our clients are 90 percent White, and I need to cater to *them*. So that interview was a complete waste of my time . . ." (8).

But the CEO involved did not originate the industry's practice of compensating advisors or her firm by how much money her advisors could get clients to invest! She just followed the crowd and then got caught saying out loud what everyone in the industry knows but keeps to themselves.

Wall Street firms occasionally reach out to recruit women and minorities. There are even annual 'Diversity Conferences', where all the big firms get together to speak of their efforts to attract women and minorities. But nothing changes. History shows that most new trainees, whatever their demographic, will not be successful anyway (9). If a firm wants to attract and keep good people, they should create and maintain good, fair policies for compensating their employees and pricing of their services; policies that are fair to employees, clients, and the public at large.

I will mention that the financial services industry does have an organization dedicated to protecting investors and safeguarding financial market integrity. That organization is the Financial Industry Regulatory Authority (FINRA). FINRA regulates investment advisors. Under FINRA is the Investor Education Foundation which provides education and useful information on saving and investing. It has available educational videos and useful financial calculators.

Also within FINRA is the Office of Financial Readiness that supports Military members and their families. Its website is: https://finred.usale-arning.gov/. FINRA is a great educational tool to help military members and their families.

A great organization, the brainchild of now Senator Elizabeth Warren, is the Consumer Financial Protection Bureau (CFPB) (https://www.consumerfinance.gov/). Every American should become familiar with the CFPB. The role of this US Government agency is to make sure the American public is treated fairly by banks, lenders, and other financial companies. The agency provides a wealth of training on many areas of personal finance and is a resource if you feel you have been wronged by a financial institution.

While these organizations provide some financial education and consumer protections, they fall short of providing the broad range of personalized financial guidance that most Americans need. The mission of FINRA is primarily to regulate *advisor* behavior, not to provide financial advice to the general public.

It might be better for the industry regulated by the government and designated to provide financial services to be rated on how well it provides those services and how many people were helped in the process. But neither of those criteria are currently being measured.

I don't propose to have all the answers to improve the current system. But perhaps a better approach in evaluating a financial advisor's contributions would be to measure: (1) the number of people helped, (2) the range and difficulty of the services provided, and (3) the financial impact of their services on the customer and his or her family? Right now the primary measurement is the dollar amount of investments sold! Ironically, the favorite reason industry leaders give for keeping the existing compensation system in place is "We would not be able to provide financial services to people with moderate income!" But taking a 5% commission on an investment from a person who doesn't have much to begin with is probably not a big help to them.

Perhaps an alternative to paying billions of dollars a year in fines and penalties for advisor misbehavior would be to provide advisors a dependable salary! That would take away the motivation to commit fraud in the first place. Also, perhaps firms could limit hiring to advisors with formal financial education and let experienced salespeople use their skills in roles of marketing and advertising. As much as people complain about the medical profession, I'm glad my doctors and nurses don't have to convince me to have surgery so they can earn a living.

Is it unreasonable to have advisor fees be calculated on how much they can *do for* customers and not how much they can *get from* customers? It will probably take Congress to change the current industry practices. So for now let's focus on what *we* can do to improve our personal finances. But before we begin the study of significant areas of finance, let's take a look at the formal financial planning process as suggested by the Board of Financial Planners.

CHAPTER 2

The Financial Planning Process

F inancial planning requires understanding certain concepts and following a process. With the wide variety in our financial resources and goals, it is not possible to have a one-size-fits-all plan or template for financial planning. But true financial planners have come up with a generalized process to follow.

The steps Certified Financial Planners™ would follow might be helpful.

1. *Gain an understanding* of your personal and financial circumstances.
2. *Identify* and *select* goals.
3. *Analyze* **current course of action** and **potential alternative** courses of action.
4. *Develop* financial planning recommendations.
5. *Present* the financial planning recommendations (document them).
6. *Implement* the financial planning recommendations; and
7. *Monitor* the progress and *update* (when necessary).

The italicized words are the action verbs in each step. Once you have achieved some financial success, I encourage you to turn to a CFP® to take your financial planning to a higher level.

Certified Financial Planners™ have a fiduciary responsibility to their clients, which means they have to put the interests of their clients ahead of their own.

Other financial professionals who have high standards and good reputations are the Chartered Financial Consultant (ChFC), Chartered Financial Analyst (CFA), Chartered Life Underwriter (CLU—Insurance), Accredited Financial Counselors (AFC), and Personal Financial Specialists—PFS (those are CPAs who specialize in financial planning).

There are many other financial professional certifications, but those are the ones that I am most familiar with that deal with *personal* financial matters. I apologize to any conscientious professionals I have overlooked. Being certified indicates a higher level of training and relevant education.

The goal of the book is not to make you a Certified Financial Planner™. But I thought there was some merit in showing you the overall process those in my profession would follow to be of help to you. If you can grasp an understanding of the most significant elements of personal finance, you will be well on your way to achieving financial independence (or financial security). A spending plan or budget is a good place to start whenever we want to improve our financial situation.

CHAPTER 3
Spending Plans (Budgeting)

"By failing to prepare, you are preparing to fail" Benjamin Franklin

Just as the spending plan is the most important element in financial planning, a positive mental attitude is the most important element in spending. We want to assume that others want our business and are willing to treat us fairly to get it (I may have to eat those words when it comes to buying cars and telephone service contracts). Your positive attitude will motivate businesspeople to want your business and inspire them to negotiate terms with you. The better you are at negotiating good terms, the better shape will be your budget and overall finances. When making purchases of significant amounts, after the seller offers a quote, ask for discounts (company specials, military, senior, student discounts, etc.)

If a discount is not possible then ask for no-interest financing. Vendors often offer no-interest financing when your purchase is above a certain dollar amount *and* you will pay the borrowed amount off within a designated time period (generally six months to two years). Obtaining concessions on significant purchases will make you feel better and have a positive impact on your finances.

The spending plan (or budget) is the most important element in financial planning. It's a picture of where we will spend money. We should break it down into individual line items, but not too small. Rounding to the nearest five dollar increment should be okay for most of us. If your gym membership is eighteen dollars per month, round up to twenty dollars. A monthly spending plan enables us to outline what is valuable to us. An Excel spreadsheet is a great help (a link is provided below).

The spending plan should show enough detail so expenditures in excess of a certain amount (15 or $20 a month) are accounted for. If you have several small expenditures that add up to a total of fifty or one hundred dollars per month, consider lumping them into *one* line item named "miscellaneous" or "other." That way your budget can likely fit on one page (one worksheet). You want to be able to see all the big things you usually spend money on and calculate whether you project a monthly surplus or deficit.

If contributions to your employer's 401K, deferred compensation plan, or other accounts are taken directly from your paycheck, it's optional to show them in your budget worksheet. Just be aware of the amounts being withheld as you estimate your monthly savings for retirement. Remember to show any ACH (automatic) deductions from your bank account for expenses or payments on loans.

A spending plan should be forward-looking. You could spend a lot of time adding small receipts and small amounts spent in the past but remember that your goal is to estimate your *future* expenses. Start with rough estimates and revise (weekly or monthly) as you learn more accurately what you spend monthly. Be sure to include rent, utilities, insurance, car payments, the big stuff.

An Excel spreadsheet is a must in composing a budget or spending plan. Excel provides a template for a budget, but make sure there are enough rows for all your larger expenses. The spreadsheet should do all the adding and subtracting for you. Tailor it to your needs. A sample is provided at my website under Services: https://guilfordtaxman.com/ . Click on the Services tab and scroll down to Budgeting. My sample allows you to forecast three months into the future. Some credit unions may also offer a budget app.

With any budget or spending plan you need to have a good grasp on how much you are actually spending from week to week in order to have a good estimate of your monthly spending. One option is to track your spending on a daily basis. When you get home in the evening you could write down how much was spent on variable expenses like gas, food, clothes, dining out, recreation, etc. Do this for a full month or two and you should have a good idea of what you are spending.

Another option is to prepare envelopes for those *variable* monthly expenses (gas, groceries, lunch, recreation, etc.) and pay for them with cash. For instance, if you think you spend $40 per week on lunch and you get paid bi-weekly, you could put $80 into a 'Lunch' envelope on pay day. If you spent $10 on lunch today, you would take $10 from the lunch envelope to replenish your purse or wallet. If after a couple of months you find there is no money in the lunch envelope before payday comes around, that indicates you are underestimating your costs for lunch. If the envelope is growing, you might be overestimating your costs for lunch. For the envelope process to work you would need to go to the bank on payday and get cash in small denominations, $5.00, $10.00, and 20 dollar bills, mostly $5.00 bills.

A final word on these variable expenses (not rent, mortgage, or the car payments which are fixed). Note that there are 4.33 weeks in each month. So converting your weekly variable expenses to monthly requires multiplying the weekly average times 4.33, not 4.00 (that's because there are 52 weeks in a year). The proof: 52 Weeks divided by 12 months = 4.33. Multiply you weekly expense by 4.33 to avoid underestimating what your variable expenses amount to monthly.

If you like to use software, there is Quicken (Simplify or Trubill if using an app). These are available for three to four dollars per month. I also see advertisements for budget management software (Personal Capital, SoFi, etc.). Just be careful not to use any investing options offered by these programs. Investing is a complicated art and science. So you wouldn't want your investments to be chosen by some budget software with arbitrary, simple, and unknown algorithms (see the detailed chapter on investing).

Another good source for budgeting and major financial guidance is the 'Financial Toolkit' from the Consumer Financial Protection Bureau (CFPB). There are over 200 pages of useful information including budget worksheets. The download is free: https://www.consumerfinance.gov/consumer-tools/educator-tools/your-money-your-goals/toolkit/

For decades, I have revised my spending plan sometimes monthly or more frequently. With the Excel spreadsheet doing the adding and subtracting, it's a small chore to update what you expect to earn and spend on average. With the three-month projection information included in my spending plan, you can see what your cash balance will be three months ahead. That way, if your spending will exceed your earnings in any one month, you can see if you will have enough cash flowing from the previous month to absorb it or whether you will need to redeem an investment or borrow to cover the shortfall.

If you are going to need to borrow money, you want to plan that borrowing ahead of time, especially if you don't have a low-interest rate credit card (or if you might be reaching your credit limit on the card). You also want to plan ahead if you will be taking any withdrawals from investments or borrowing against your 401K or permanent life insurance policy. It's not a good idea to sell stocks during a down stock market, and you need to know in advance whether you can even borrow against the 401K or insurance policy. A **big** mistake is to take *withdrawals* from your retirement accounts before age 59 & 1/2 (so borrowing against it is preferable). Taking out money before you reach 59 & ½ could result in you paying 40 percent of your withdrawal in federal and state income taxes (with the 10-percent tax penalty). The same could happen with a life insurance policy or an annuity (see the in-depth chapters on life insurance and annuities).

We should embrace spending plans. It is better to plan what you will be spending than to spend haphazardly and hope we spent well (effectively, timely, and economically).

Budgeting has become more challenging with the widespread use of credit cards and debit cards. Even if you use a credit card to regularly pay for certain monthly expenses, you should still capture the expense in your spending plan so you can know whether you are operating with a budget surplus or deficit. And if you have to carry a balance on your credit card, consider adding a line item for the (average) monthly interest expense you are being charged. That way, you will see the true cost of your monthly expenses and be motivated to pay the card balance down.

A potential challenge today is the so-called "Financial Technology" Companies affiliating with employers to allow employees access to their "accrued" wages prior to payday. They are probably bankrolled by the Pay Day Loan industry and some large banks. Their fees for these services have been quoted at six dollars per transaction. That is a lot of money for the convenience of getting some of your money before payday. There are probably other fees involved that merchants might add.

One major bank is already advertising, "Get *your paycheck ahead of time.*" In any case, don't allow these companies access to your paycheck before payday. It would be better to rely on a low interest major credit card (Visa, Discover, etc.) that you can get through your credit union. If you can budget well, you can wait until payday. When I audited the State of Oklahoma in 1990, I found that state employees were only paid once a month. So those state employees had to become good at budgeting and planning their financial activities. I still have a great "Sooners" sweatshirt with a covered wagon on the front. I did not mention the Nebraska football team during that assignment. Next chapter we will discuss goal setting.

CHAPTER 4

Financial Goal Setting and Strategies

Once we have prepared our spending plan (or budget), the next step is to define some goals. Later we will design some tactics and strategies to achieve them. In that process, be prepared to update your budget after establishing goals and determining how much per month you want to spend or save to accomplish them.

Your age, ambitions, responsibilities, and resources all influence the goals you set. Robert S. Rubin from St. Louis University coined the acronym, SMART, to assist us in defining our goals. Writing down a goal increases our chances of achieving it. The letters of the acronym stand for:

Specific – Measurable – Attainable – Relevant – Time-Based

Some examples are:

Specific -   Buy a car for cash in twenty-four months (we know cash is a great bargaining tool).
Measurable -   Accumulate $12,000.
Attainable -   Yes, I can put away $500 per month.
Relevant -   Satisfies the need for necessary and convenient transportation
Time-based -   Goal to be achieved in twenty-four months

Another example:

Specific -	Pay off credit cards in twenty-four months.
Measurable -	Pay off $12,000 balance.
Attainable -	Yes, I can pay $554 per month (factoring in interest at 10 percent)
Relevant -	Improves finances and credit score
Time-based -	Goal to be achieved in twenty-four months

Other goals might be:

- ✓ Saving for retirement (the ultimate goal);
- ✓ Saving for education;
- ✓ Buying permanent life insurance or a burial policy;
- ✓ Saving for a down payment on a house;
- ✓ Starting a business; or
- ✓ Planning a wedding or vacation

Some goals require extensive planning (like retirement and saving for education), but do not agonize if you can't check off *all* five criteria in the SMART acronym. The SMART acronym is a good tool to outline your goals when you can. It helps to know where you are going, so you can design a route to get there. Accomplishing more than one goal can be challenging.

Goals taken in isolation are devoid of financial planning. We must prioritize these goals and come up with strategies to achieve them. But in the process of prioritizing, you may find it necessary to compromise. Compromising with the goal that has the least positive impact on your finances is a rational choice.

One way of compromising would be to work a little towards each goal. Or you might even weigh your priorities and apply percentages of your savings toward each goal every month (the highest priority getting most money). Or you could work to achieve the most important goal first, then work on the one of next importance, and so on. Neither approach is right or wrong as long as you do not incur avoidable expenses, forgo significant opportunities for earnings, or miss important deadlines necessary to achieve an important goal.

Income taxes are next. If you live on a tight budget, a tax savings or tax credit could add to your available cash and assist in achieving your financial goals. Be sure to revise your budget to include any expected tax savings. With a little experience and effort, you can estimate the amount of your potential tax refunds or taxes owed as the year progresses. You don't want to owe a lot when it is time to file, but you don't want to get enormous refunds either. Instead of getting giant refunds, you could put that money in the bank to earn some interest. Perhaps you could plan to limit your expected refunds to no more than one month's earnings or spending? If you project a refund higher than one month's earnings (or expenses) have a little less taxes withheld. **But put the extra money in the bank— don't spend it! Don't put yourself into a position where you cannot pay your taxes!**

There are some ways people in the middle and low-income tax brackets can benefit from the tax laws, but not enough elite financial advisors address the needs of people with middle and low incomes. So let us begin here.

CHAPTER 5
Income Tax Saving Strategies

Taxes it's been said is the Price We Pay for Civilization

There are always a few areas of tax relief for those living with middle or low incomes. You will benefit from the help of a qualified, reasonable tax preparer. If the preparer is worth his or her salt, they should be able to justify their fee by showing you tax-saving strategies or deductions and credits you may not know of. A referral from a trusted friend or associate is a good way to find someone. I prefer using CPAs when their prices are reasonable. If they are both a CPA and CFP®, they can help with your taxes and help improve your finances too.

Because tax laws change every year, I chose to focus on tax items that have had consistent Congressional support. I will limit detailed calculations since dollar amounts of deductions and credits change yearly. To check the current status of the deductions and credits below, go to https://www.IRS.gov/. My goal here is to introduce you to helpful deductions and credits and strategies to make the best of them.

Listed below are some tax laws and regulations that 99 percent of us can benefit from:

1. Earned Income Credit (Schedule EIC)
2. Child Tax Credit (form 2441 and sometimes form 8812)
3. Child & Dependent Care Expense Credit (form 2441)

4. Home Mortgage Interest and Property Taxes (Schedule A or Schedule E)
5. Retirement Contributions (taxes can be deferred with a Traditional IRA or tax-free with a Roth)
6. Saver's Credit (a credit for low-income earners who contribute to a retirement plan)
7. Education (tax-free savings and tax credits [Form 8863])
8. Capital gains taxes (lower rates than ordinary income tax rates [Schedule D])
9. Business Activities (self-employment [Schedule C, E, Forms 1120, 1120S])
10. Property Tax or Rent Paid Credits for Low Income or Seniors (check your state and county)
11. Residential Energy/Solar Energy Credit; and
12. IRA Tax strategies

Some deductions and credits may also be discussed in detail in other chapters like Retirement, Education, and Investing.

Pay special attention to *credits* because they are dollar-for-dollar adjustments against your tax liability. In some cases, a credit may even be "refundable," meaning you will get a cash refund even if the credit exceeds your tax liability.

Deductions are not as valuable as credits. Deductions may save you a percentage of the amount of the deduction. The savings depends upon your tax bracket. So if your effective tax rate is 20 percent, a one-hundred-dollar tax deduction will save you twenty dollars. On the other hand if you got a *credit* for one hundred dollars, you might get one hundred dollars in tax savings or an additional $100 in your tax refund. So both deductions and credits are good, but tax credits are usually better.

Earned Income Credit (EIC): For a person with low to moderate income who has a dependent child, this credit can amount to thousands of dollars a year. The credit is even available if you have an adult dependent who is disabled. There is even a small EIC for single taxpayers. For

2021, taxpayers were qualified for the credit with adjusted gross incomes as high as $57,400 (if they were married with three children). The amount of the credit ranged from $543 if you had no children to $6,728 with three qualifying children.

Child Tax Credit: The Child Tax Credit (not to be confused with the *childcare* credit) can result in a credit of between 2,000 and $2,500, for each qualifying child under the age of seventeen. In June 2021, the maximum amount was increased to $3,600 for children five and under, and $3,000 for children aged six or above (as long as they don't turn seventeen during the year). Beginning in June 2021, the Internal Revenue Service (IRS) may pay half the total credit amount monthly in advance. The dollar amounts of the credit are frequently changed by Congress.

Two circumstances can cause your credit to "phase out" or be eliminated. (1) You have no tax liability (even so, you may be able to get up to $1,400 back with the *Additional* Child Tax Credit), **or** (2) your adjusted gross income (AGI) is too high. In 2021, the maximum AGI before phasing out completely (resulting in no credit) was $150,000 for married filing jointly or qualifying widower; $112,000 if head of household; and $75,000 if single or married filing separately.

The qualifying child may have been adopted but must still be under seventeen at the end of the year. They also must be a citizen or resident of the U.S. *and* claimed as a dependent. They can be your child, a descendent, or brother or sister. Foster children are eligible too. The Child Tax Credit is claimed on Form 2441.

The *Additional Child Tax Credit* can come into play if you can't claim the full amount of the Child Tax Credit. This credit can be up to $1,400 (and will be adjusted for inflation). This credit is "refundable," meaning it can be received even if you have no tax liability. The credit is claimed on Form 8812. *You will need the dependent's social security number or an Individual's Tax Identification Number (ITIN) for either the child tax credit or the additional child tax credit.*

Child and Dependent Care Expense Credit: The Child and Dependent Care Credit may be available for expenses you paid for the care of a child (or qualified person) while you worked (or looked for work). The calculations are complicated, so we'll focus mostly on who, what, and how to qualify for the credit.

A "qualifying person" can be a child, other than your child, as long as he or she is a dependent and was under thirteen when care was provided for him or her. Your spouse can even be a qualifying person if he or she was physically or mentally unable to care for themselves. The qualifying person must have lived with you for more than half the year.

The payments for care could have even been made to a relative, as long as they were nineteen or older by the end of the year—and are *not* your dependent.

The qualifying expenses normally do not include food, clothing, education, or entertainment. But small amounts incidental to the care that cannot be separated from the cost of care may be acceptable.

This credit can be for expenses incurred while looking for work. If you had no employment but your spouse was working, on a joint tax return there may be enough earned income to still use the credit.

Self-employed persons may also claim this credit, whether you worked full time or part time.

You will need to provide the taxpayer identification number (TIN) or social security number of the person providing the care. Their names and addresses are needed to complete Form 2441. This is important because the IRS requires due diligence on your part to get this information. Without due diligence, the IRS could deny the credit. If necessary, use Form W-10 to request the required information from the care provider and keep a copy for your records.

If the provider refuses to provide the information, you can list his or her name and address or whatever information you have on the front of Form 2441 and write "See page 2." Then on page 2, near the bottom of the form, explain that you asked for the information but the provider refused to give it. That should help satisfy the due diligence requirement.

The childcare credit can be up to $8,000 for the care of one qualifying person or $16,000 for two or more persons. The calculations are based on a sliding scale using your adjusted gross income (AGI). At the lower end of the scale, an AGI of 0 to $125,000 might allow you 50 percent of the childcare expense. At the upper end of the income scale, an AGI of $438,000 or higher would allow you to a credit of *zero percent* of the childcare expenses.

For example, let's say your AGI was more than $125,000 and your childcare expenses were $10,000, your credit would be $5,000 (50 percent of $10,000). Because of the phase out, if someone's AGI was $185,000 and they had $20,000 in childcare expenses, their credit would be $4,000 (*20 percent of $20,000*).

Congress routinely changes the AGI limits for the child tax credits and childcare credits. They may increase or decrease the maximum credits. If you have children or care for a disabled dependent, the child credit and childcare credit can be very helpful.

The Home Mortgage Interest and Property Taxes: These expenses are deducted on Schedule A for your primary residence and one vacation home (or Schedule E for properties you rent to others). Deductible state and local taxes were limited to $10,000 for the years 2019–2025 on Schedule A. For the same period, the standard deduction has been raised to $24,000 for married filing jointly, $18,000 for head of household, and $12,000 for single folks. The $10,000 limit on state and local taxes may not have been an issue for you unless you lived in California, New York, or another high property tax state and your state taxes were higher than your standard deduction.

After 2025, if Congress is not as generous with the standard deductions *and* removes the $10,000 limitation on deducting state and local taxes, the amounts paid for mortgage interest and property taxes may again become a helpful deduction on Schedule A. If these expenses are paid on properties you rent to others, the deductions are taken on Schedule E, without regard for the standard deduction or the $10,000 limitation for state and local taxes.

Retirement Contributions: A tax deduction can be taken using a *Traditional* IRA. A tax deduction can also be taken for contributions to 401Ks and deferred compensation plans. Contributions to a *Roth* IRA or

Roth 401Ks are not deductible. See the chapter on retirement for additional information.

Saver's Credit: This is an extra credit for low to moderate-income earners who contribute to a retirement plan (IRAs, 401Ks, etc.). It is often forgotten or overlooked. See below and the chapter on retirement for additional information.

Education: Earnings on investments made for educational purposes can be tax-free. On top of that, education tax credits can result in even more tax savings. For instance, the American Opportunity Credit is available for the first four years of college and the Lifetime Learning Credit (a smaller figure) is available after the American Opportunity Credit is used up. The Lifetime Learning Credit is available no matter how many years of college you have completed (more details in the chapter on education).

Capital Gains Taxes: Tax rates for capital gains are usually lower than the "ordinary" income tax rates we pay on our salaries and income from other sources. Investments held for one year or longer receive the *long-term* capital gains tax rate. The chapter on investments goes into more detail.

Business Activities (Self-Employment): Most expenses incurred while doing business are tax-deductible (although meals and entertainment are usually limited to 50 percent of the amounts paid). An individual who is a sole proprietor customarily reports their income on Schedule C while corporations report their income and expenses on Form 1120 or 1120(S). Sub Chapter S corporations and partnerships pass their income or losses through to our personal income tax returns. An LLC (Limited Liability Company) may choose to use a Schedule C. The LLC may file as a corporation *after* approval from the IRS. Requests to file as an S Corporation must be submitted to the IRS by the fifteenth day of the second month in the organization's tax year (March 15 for calendar-year organizations). More discussion can be found in the chapter on business.

Property Tax or Rent Payment Credits: Often, your state or county will offer low-income and senior citizens a credit for property taxes or rents paid. For instance, in Arizona, if someone over sixty-five (or disabled) had earnings of less than $3,751 ($5,501 if someone lived with them), they could receive a tax refund for a portion of the property tax or rent they paid. Many states offer the same option and it is often addressed on the state income tax return (hopefully the income limits are higher than they are in Arizona). Some states require that the form be filed by April 15, so you could lose the benefit if you file an extension for the tax year of your claim.

Some states or counties may allow you to "freeze" the assessment on your property when you are sixty-five or older. That would be a good idea if your income becomes fixed or if your income falls. Significant increases in property taxes can be a heavy burden to senior citizens. Be sure you submit documents by the required date.

Residential Energy/Solar Energy Credit: There has been an ongoing credit of 10 percent of the cost of energy efficiency improvements to owner occupied residential property. The credit is limited to $200, $300, or $500, depending upon the type of property (windows, water heater, fans, etc.). A larger credit is the Residential Energy Efficient Property Credit (REEP). For qualified solar, fuel cell, wind, and geothermal heat, the credit is 26 percent of the cost for property placed in service in 2021 and 2022. However the Inflation Reduction Act of 2022 may have re-instated the credit to 30% (the original amount). Any credit not used may be carried forward for three years. The credit is set to phase out beginning in 2033. Many states also have a residential energy credit.

Some Theory on IRAs and 401K Plans. With a Traditional IRA, you get a tax deduction in the current year and postpone income taxes on the contribution and the earnings until withdrawals are taken. But with a Roth IRA, you don't get a tax deduction now with your contribution, but you may get tax-free income on the earnings in the future. You can even contribute to both in the same year (just be sure the combined contributions stay within the *total* IRS allowable limits for IRAs for the year—you can't double up).

The benefit to having both a Roth and Traditional IRA set up is you can choose which one to contribute to depending upon your income in that year. If you don't expect to be in a higher tax bracket during retirement, then in the years you don't earn very much, your contributions to a

Traditional IRA might provide you more cash by deducting the IRA contribution (just don't create *negative* taxable income. Remember your standard deduction and exemptions also reduce your taxable income). Rather than create negative taxable income, you could contribute some to the Roth IRA. In years when your income is higher than your living needs (when you have a budget surplus), contribute to the Roth IRA to enjoy tax-free income in the future.

By contributing to either type of IRA, 401K, etc., the Retirement Savers Credit could create additional tax savings. The credit phases out for couples with income above $68,000, $51,000 for head of households, and $34,000 for single filers (these upper limits are for the 2022 tax year). The Savers Credit provides a great opportunity for low-income earners to build a source of income during retirement. Contributions to Roth IRAs and 401ks entitle you to the savers credit too.

Advisors may present illustrations showing that a Roth IRA is superior because you would enjoy tax-free income in future years. But these illustrations assume you have sufficient money to fund a Roth IRA and that you will be in a higher tax bracket during retirement. If your income is limited now and you are on a tight budget, why not take the opportunity to save taxes by using a Traditional IRA now since you could use the extra money (Just don't make your taxable income go negative). When your taxable income reaches zero—you won't get a larger refund if your taxable income goes negative!

For low-to-middle-income retirees, the combination of the standard deduction and personal tax exemptions during retirement could result in most of their Traditional IRA distributions coming out tax-free! So you would have had the benefit of the Traditional IRA tax deduction in your working years and were then able to take the money out tax-free (or at the lowest tax rates) during retirement. Along the same line of thinking, it does not make sense to contribute to a Roth IRA if you will have to borrow money for living expenses!

The maximum allowable income thresholds to contribute to Roth IRAs are much higher than for Traditional IRAs. For either IRAs, the maximum income thresholds are higher for couples who file jointly than for single taxpayers. If you do *not* have a retirement plan at work, you can contribute to an IRA no matter how high your income is. Except income limits still apply if your spouse has a retirement plan at work, but those income limits will be higher since *both* spouses did not have retirement plans at work.

Roth IRAs are popular because you might get tax-free distributions of earnings in retirement. Also, with Roth IRAs, you will not be required to take mandatory minimum withdrawals at age seventy-two as with a Traditional IRA (Congress may change that to age 75). If you don't need a tax deduction now and expect to be in a high tax bracket in retirement, you would definitely benefit from the Roth IRA.

If you will be in a lower tax bracket in retirement but are paying high taxes now, you will want to use the Traditional IRA (assuming your income is not so high that you don't qualify to take a deduction for the Traditional IRA). If so, you may still qualify to contribute to a Roth.

The following are the maximum Modified Adjusted Gross Income (MAGI) thresholds for contributing to Traditional and Roth IRAs for 2021. An IRA contribution phases out completely between MAGI:

	Married Filing Jointly	Single
Traditional IRAs	$105,000–$125,000	$66,000–$76,000
Roth IRAs	$66,000–$208,000	$125,000–$140,000

The maximum IRA contributions allowed per person in 2021 is $6,000. You may contribute an additional $1,000 if you are over age fifty. Please go to the IRS charts at IRS.gov to see the limits if you do *not* have a retirement plan at work but your spouse does and you are filing jointly (https://irs.gov). It does take some thought to decide which type of IRA contribution will benefit you more.

Also, do not make a *non-deductible* contribution to an IRA or 401K (i.e., you earned too much to contribute). Non-deductible contributions will require that you classify a portion of *every* distribution you take in retirement as taxable and non-taxable for the rest of your life!

Let's say 75% of your retirement savings was in taxable IRAs and 401ks and 25% was in Roth and Non-deductible IRA accounts. For the rest of your life, 75% of the money you take out of your accounts will be taxable and 25% will not be taxable. Besides the headache of figuring your taxable and non-taxable income each year, this could hamper your investment strategies and budgeting efforts. Even as an accountant, it would stress me to have to calculate the percentage of my withdrawals that were taxable for the rest of my life. It would be like agreeing to take medication for the rest of your life to deal with a temporary headache when you could just as easily have taken a day of rest! Better options would be to put the additional investment into a brokerage (individual) account or in a permanent life insurance policy.

Your employer's match on a 401K is considered "free money." Even if you are on a tight budget, you will want to get your employer's match—at least up to the maximum the employer will match. Let's say your employer will match up to 2 percent of your salary, and you earn $50,000 per year. For your $1,000 contribution, your employer will match another $1,000.

Even if contributing the $1,000 is difficult, consider that your *out-of-pocket* cost might only be **$630** after tax deductions and tax credits. For example: if you were married and, in the 15 percent federal tax bracket with a state tax rate of 2 percent, your combined tax rate would be 17 percent. The contribution then allows you to save $170 since the $1,000 was deducted from your gross income (17 percent times $1,000 = $170). But you might also get to use the Savers credit!

By use of the Saver's Credit (Form 8880), you can save an additional $200 (20 percent times $1,000). So you would be out of pocket only $630 ($1,000 less $170 less $200). You now have $2,000 invested in a retirement account and growing, and it only cost you $630 ($1,000 came from your employer). What a great return on a $630 investment! (And that's before it starts to grow).

Whether you make a Roth or Traditional IRA contribution, be sure to check whether you are entitled to the Saver's Tax Credit. This can be a tremendous benefit if your income is low. Also, if you are doing your own taxes, it's best to enter a Roth contribution into your tax software. Even though the Roth is not deductible, the contribution should trigger the Saver's Credit and provide documentation for the future.

Be careful of taking money out of your IRA or 401K prematurely (before age 59 & 1/2). Even a person in the middle-income brackets can pay **40 percent** in taxes on the premature distributions of pensions or life insurance products. Consider the person in the 25 percent federal tax bracket who gets hit with a 10 percent penalty for early withdrawals. Add state income taxes at 5 percent, and he or she would have a tax liability of nearly 40 percent of the withdrawal! If you filed those tax returns late, nearly half of your withdrawal would need to be paid out to the IRS and the state because of added interest and penalties. (The penalty was temporarily waived on 2020 tax returns because of the coronavirus)!

Some 401K plans will allow you to borrow against your account, but it has to be repaid within five years. That is still a much better option than taking a premature withdrawal and paying out 40 percent of it in taxes and penalties.

Exceptions to the 10 Percent Penalty for Early Withdrawals: I don't like to plan on using exceptions, but just in case you need money from your retirement plan unexpectedly before age 59 & 1/2, you may be able to avoid the 10-percent penalty if the withdrawal was under the following circumstances:

1. Used for the taxpayer, spouse, child, or grandchild's higher education
2. For a first-time home buyer, up to $10,000 (first time can mean you haven't owned a home in two years)
3. In the event of a permanent disability
4. To satisfy a Qualified Domestic Relations Order (QDRO)
5. To pay for qualifying medical expenses
6. To pay for health insurance when unemployed

7. With separation from public service after age fifty-five
8. Received as a result of the death of a plan participant (you inherited an IRA, 401k, etc.); or
9. Rollovers to another qualified plan are exceptions too. *Direct* rollovers are best. If the rollover is not direct (trustee to trustee) and *you* receive a check, 20 percent will be withheld for taxes, *and* you still have to put 100 percent of the requested amount into the new fund to avoid paying the tax (and potential penalty).

If receiving withdrawals in annual installments will work for you, there is an option to avoid the 10 percent penalty under Code Section 72T of the Internal Revenue Code. You would need to take "substantially equal periodic payments" for at least five years or until age 59 & 1/2 if that is longer. The dollar amount of the payments you would receive would be based upon your life expectancy (using the IRS tables) with the "Fixed" method or the "Amortization" method.

Another option under Code Section 72T is to "annuitize" the payments. But if you choose this option, you will *not* be able to change the distribution payment amount later as you would with the first two options above. The first two options allow you to alter your withdrawals after age 59 & 1/2 or five years (whichever is longer). The 72T election might be helpful if you are age fifty or more and just need to supplement your income for a few years before you reach 59 & 1/2.

If you were fortunate enough not to need much of your Traditional IRA or Traditional 401K account and you turn age seventy-two, you will need to begin taking required minimum distributions (RMD) by April 1 of the year *following* the year you turn seventy-two. These distributions must begin for the IRS wants you to take money out and pay taxes on it. Subsequent distributions must be taken by December 31 of each year. The amount you must take out each year is determined by the IRA or 401k plan administrator and they will send you notifications of the amount. In 2022, Congress was making an effort to raise the age for RMDs from 72 to 75. (RMDs do not apply to Roth IRAs or Roth 401ks).

You only need to take a portion of the "total" of all the traditional IRAs and 401k accounts to satisfy RMDs. Let's say you have $300,000 in total traditional IRA balances spread among three mutual funds, and each plan administrator writes and says you need to take out $5,000 during the year. You can take $15,000 from only one of the IRAs and still be in compliance with your total RMD for the year. You don't need to take $5,000 from each mutual fund company; you only need to take out a total of $15,000.

That's good to know because if your stock mutual fund investments are down, you may want to leave them alone and take money from your *bond* funds or other fixed investment accounts. So if you are going to be aggressive with your traditional IRAs by being heavy in stocks or stock mutual funds, you should still have some bond funds available to withdraw your RMD if the market happens to be down most of the year.

On the other hand, if your stock mutual funds are doing very well (say, they had a 13 percent or more increase in value during the year), you may want to take most of the $15,000 RMD from some combination of the stock mutual funds. That would leave your bond funds to be available for future safety (these ideas are covered more in the chapters on investments and retirement).

Why all the fuss about RMD? The tax penalty for not taking out the required minimum distribution is **50 percent** of the amount that should have been taken out! So **do not** overlook the RMD. If your plan was to leave most of the IRA to a younger beneficiary, a Roth IRA would have been a better choice. So if you have a traditional IRA that you want to leave to someone, it would be cheaper to make a Roth conversion and pay taxes on the Roth conversion than to ignore the RMD requirements. Just like taxes, insurance can have a significant impact on our finances.

CHAPTER 6

Insurance (Sharing Risks, What Kind and How Much?)

E ven though I have been an insurance agent for several years, I often thought of insurance as an expense to be minimized (I tolerated life, auto, disability, professional liability, and homeowner's insurance). But after experiencing Hurricane Katrina and our home was destroyed, I began to appreciate the role of insurance more. We should look at insurance as an investment to protect what is valuable to us.

You can buy health insurance, long-term care, business interruption, umbrella insurance policies, and more. Disability insurance can also be of value when you have responsibilities to others and they depend upon your ability to provide income.

Insurance is a matter of sharing risk with other parties, particularly insurance companies. The questions to ask of yourself are: Where are you most at risk and what risks would you like to pass on to an insurance company? What premiums can you afford? Following are some features and provisions of certain types of insurance and some theory to help you decide which to buy.

Life Insurance: Life insurance covers the risk that you will not live long enough to provide for those who depend on you. There are basically two types—term insurance and permanent insurance. Term insurance is more popular, and premiums are less than the premiums on permanent life insurance. With term insurance (over five, ten, or twenty years), you contract for insurance on your life, and if you die during the term, your beneficiaries receive the face amount of the policy.

Permanent life insurance is more complicated. There are several types: Whole Life, Universal Life, Variable Life, and more. Permanent insurance is more expensive because you expect to build up cash value, and that cash value may be used for different things.

Some term insurance policies have a *convertible* feature that allows conversion to a permanent policy later on without proof of insurability. The convertible option would be nice in case you can later afford a permanent policy. *Renewability* is a desirable feature that enables the insured to get continued coverage without providing proof of insurability.

With permanent insurance, part of the premium goes toward your life insurance (pure insurance), and the rest of the premium is used to grow cash value. The *premium in excess of the cost of insurance* may build up cash value if certain provisions are met. Each type of permanent insurance has different features, and insurance companies may add riders and provisions that may be appealing to you.

Interest as used in this discussion may mean the interest the insurance company earns (for itself) from investing in bonds. Interest (or dividends) in this discussion can also mean what the insurance company pays *you* to increase your cash value. Insurance agents may present illustrations that project the future performance the policies *may* pay you later under different scenarios.

Policy illustrations are basically projections of future performance. They are the drawing boards for what can be expected long-term from a particular permanent policy. An illustration summarizes the policy and contains numeric information, including the death benefit, premium payments, projected cash value, and so on. Some items in the illustrations are guaranteed, and some are not. When an item in an illustration may vary or is contingent on outside factors, it is **not** guaranteed. Ask the insurance agent to explain, "How will the policy projections be affected if interest rates rise?" "What if interest rates fall?" In general, the more aggressive the assumptions in the illustrations and the more flexible the policy, the more volatile (affected) the policy will be by changes in expenses and future interest rates.

Four questions to ask before buying a permanent insurance policy are:

1. Does it fit into my budget?
2. What additional benefit am I trying to insure or provide with the buildup of cash value?
3. Is there potential for a good rate of return on my money? and
4. What is the probability (risk) that I will need some or all of the cash values before age 59 & 1/2?

Permanent insurance can be good for younger people if they can afford the higher premiums. That's because a smaller part of the total premium paid goes toward life insurance so more of the premium is building cash value. Unfortunately, many young people can't afford the higher premiums. You usually can't make withdrawals of your cash value before age 59 & ½ without a tax penalty (sometimes a policy may allow loans against the cash value after a certain term, possibly twenty years).

Because both permanent life insurance policies and annuities are provided by insurance companies, they are sometimes compared, but they are for two different purposes. Life insurance provides money to your heirs if you *die*. Annuities can provide *you* with income after your working years. There is a full chapter in the book on annuities.

It is important to think of what *you* want as the insurance agent lists all the things a permanent insurance policy can do. Consider whether your income is stable enough and whether you will be able to continue your commitment to the policy long-term or for the periods used in the illustrations? If the bottom line rate of return (profitability) you would get from the insurance contract is less than you could get if you invested the additional premium in the stock market yourself, you may want to pass on the permanent life policy and go with term insurance instead. Just be sure you *invest* the difference in premiums that you save. There are several types of permanent life policies with different attractions and provisions.

With a **Traditional Whole life** insurance policy, you may pay fixed level premiums until age one hundred. Dividends (interest) are paid on the premiums, and the pure insurance cost decreases over time as the cash value increases. Some policies may have the option of increasing the face value of the policy (the death Benefit) after so much is paid in. On cash withdrawals, owners pay taxes only on the excess over the total premiums paid.

Limited Pay Life policies are similar to traditional whole life policies except premiums cease at the end of a set period. Insurance coverage remains, but no more premiums are required. Because periods are shorter than the one hundred years on the traditional whole life policy, annual premiums are usually higher.

Current Assumption Whole Life (CAWL) has a fixed premium schedule and level death benefit. You receive a guaranteed minimum interest rate and a guaranteed minimum cash value. But at regular intervals (five or ten years), the policy is reevaluated. If the interest rates the insurance company earned on its bonds have been better than anticipated, and mortality rates better than expected (that is fewer covered people died), you would be given the chance to reduce your premiums. Or you could increase the death benefit or cash value.

With **Universal Life insurance**, the insurance company credits your account with interest income (on the part of the premium in excess of the insurance cost). It will have a *flexible* premium, and the death benefit may be fixed or increased. The flexible premium allows the owner to pay in more than the stated premium. The interest paid to you is based on the guaranteed interest rate (3–4 percent) plus any excess interest the insurance company declares. Universal life policies are sometimes used as a wealth accumulator. Premiums may be skipped as long as there is enough cash value to pay for the pure insurance. It is like a savings account except the interest rates paid will usually be higher. But there is usually a back-end sales load (a service charge for early policy surrenders). Withdrawals can be made that reduce the death benefit.

Indexed Universal Life Insurance. With the decline in interest rates over the past 15 or so years, Indexed Universal Life Insurance policies became popular. The rate of interest paid is based upon a market index like the S&P 500 or the 10-Year US Treasury index. As the index moves up, the policy will be credited with a percentage of the increase. If the index moves down, the policy will not be credited with interest, but the cash value will not be reduced. The difference between Indexed and traditional Universal Life Insurance is how the insurance company credits interest (income) to the policy. There is a guaranteed rate (like the Universal Life Policy except it is usually lower), but it also has an index participation rate, and the crediting process for the interest and rates are extremely complicated.

If you are interested in an Indexed Universal Life policy, have agents from competing companies run illustrations, using the same premium payments under similar and different (projected) market conditions. That way you can see which policy would result in higher returns under certain circumstances. Now that the Federal Reserve has raised interest rates in 2022, I suspect these policies will pay higher interest rates (to begin with). Finally, there are even three different options on how the death benefit will be calculated. Universal life policies will have less risk than Variable Life Insurance policies.

A **Variable Life Insurance** policy is similar to a whole life policy since the premiums remain fixed. The difference is the premium paid in excess of the insurance cost is usually invested in stock or bond mutual funds. There is a guaranteed death benefit that will vary with the values of the investment accounts. Loans may be taken against a large percentage of the cash value. The policy may lapse if premiums are not paid or when loans exceed the cash value.

With a **Variable *Universal* Life insurance** policy (**VUL**), the premiums may be fixed **or** flexible. The insurance company pays interest on the excess of the premium over the cost of your life insurance. Premium options may vary. You might pay nothing one month and then the following month pay the maximum allowed by the IRS! The policy holder assumes the risk that the cash values will grow with a VUL while the insurance company assumes the growth risk with *whole life* and *universal life* policies. There is a guaranteed minimum death benefit. You may choose sub accounts that are tied to the stock or bond market. Understand that these sub-accounts are subject to stock or bond market ups and downs with no guarantees of return of principal.

A VUL policy may be a good option for someone who wants potential stock market earnings over the long term, wants to defer income taxes on those earnings, and has maxed out his or her IRA or 401K contributions. The VUL may be good for a younger person who can afford the premiums and doesn't mind stock market risk. Be sure you won't need to touch the money before you are age 59 & ½. VULs will have expenses for sales and administration costs. These costs may be deducted up front or at the back end of the policy.

If you purchase insurance from a *mutual* insurance company, it will likely be a "participating" policy. With participation, you are eligible to receive a dividend or policy refund. The dividends reflect the difference between the insurance company's actual costs (claims and expenses) and the premiums collected. Options for receiving the dividend include paying future premiums for you, receiving a cash refund, or purchasing more death benefit.

Life insurance can be useful in estate planning. It's a good way to provide potentially tax-free income for your heirs and create equal value in inheritance (i.e. one child gets the house, and another child gets more life insurance proceeds).

If you are married, and social security is a significant part of family income, be sure to ask the Social Security Administration how much benefits will be reduced if you or your spouse pass away. The amount of monthly social security death benefits a spouse will be paid is important (I'm not speaking of the little one-time death benefit payment of $255). The amount of life insurance purchased should take into consideration the potential loss of social security benefits. A surviving spouse who did not work could lose as much as one-third of the benefit. If both spouses were workers, the surviving spouse could lose as much as 50 percent of his or her benefit.

An option for a couple is to purchase a *first to die* whole life insurance policy. Both lives are insured under the same policy. The surviving spouse will receive an insurance benefit, no matter which spouse passes first.

Insuring Children: No amount of life insurance can replace a child. The primary reason to carry life insurance on a child is to get non-cancelable insurance coverage in place. This would be a blessing later in life if the child (as a teenager or adult) is diagnosed with an uninsurable condition. Provisions like *guaranteed renewable* and *increasing coverage* are great for an individual who would otherwise not qualify for life insurance. It would be a good strategy to insure children with a policy with a manageable premium or a smaller face value than to pass up this insurance altogether.

How much life insurance do you need? The older calculation was the Human Value Method—where you estimated how much a bread winner would have provided had he or she lived. A better approach is the Needs Analysis Method. The needs analysis method emphasizes how much the *beneficiaries* are going to need. But there is more to consider before we go to the insurance calculator.

A younger bread winner will need more insurance than an older person with more financial assets. Also, adult children might need less support than minors. A sole bread winner in a household would need more insurance than a two-earner household. The younger the beneficiaries, the more insurance you should buy.

Consider whether you are trying to provide for both your spouse and children or just your children. Are you trying to provide for college education only, or college *and* support until age thirty? Answers to these questions will help you answer the question on some insurance calculators, "How many years of income do you need?" The age of the insured person would be factored in also. It would be best to perform some calculations on your own before speaking with an insurance agent. With the above in mind, let's go to the insurance calculator: https://www.bankrate.com/calculators/insurance/life-insurance-calculator.aspx.

Final Expenses: Senior citizens who are single may reach a point in life where insurance coverage is no longer a necessity but there are still some expenses involved in ones passing. Their children might be grown and independent, and the house may be paid off, but they still need to cover final expenses. Social Security will only pay a one-time death benefit of $255! The average funeral costs are about $8,000 and luckily, funeral costs have not risen substantially over the years. A good option is a pre-paid burial policy with a reputable funeral home. That will allow you to pay ahead for the service and not have to worry about rising costs. Don't forget to consider final medical expenses and legal fees. The value of a prepaid burial policy may also be excluded from "counted assets" when needing to qualify for long-term care under Medicaid.

Military Veterans may want to look into Veteran's funeral arrangements. You don't have to be a combat Veteran and you are not limited to military cemeteries. Burial policies are a good form of insurance. But there are even more insurance products to consider, and long-term care is a big one.

CHAPTER 7

Long Term Care (LTC) Insurance

To some, long-term care might sound like care provided to senior citizens in a hospital or nursing home, but a lot more is involved. My focus used to be on how you would deal with the high cost of long-term care while protecting your savings. But I have learned there are several venues for care and different levels of care. As regarding the costs of care, seniors face a juggling act involving their resources, the government's interest, and the interests of the insurance companies.

We should weigh each party's interest in the cost of LTC . We also need to consider our potential need for care, levels of insurance coverage, and desired types of care. This chapter will consider more than just the cost of LTC insurance. If you are fifty or older, please read carefully.

Preparing for long-term care is more complicated than just buying an LTC insurance policy. We also need to answer the question: How do we wish to live as we age? Most of us don't even want to think about aging so it's hard to think about options for living as an older version of ourselves. Much of that mindset is based on how older people are perceived in American society. Few movie stars, models, athletes, or CPAs begin their careers after age thirty. We even discriminate against ourselves, not wanting to admit to being a member of AARP. I joined as soon as I was old enough! I thought of it as moving on to another chapter of my life. If you don't know what AARP stands for, that's okay, you will learn in time.

Given our varied circumstances and many choices for living as seniors, it is difficult to recommend one or two courses of action. I think it is important to discuss different options for insurance, options for senior living, and the options for care. I chose to address Medicaid toward the end of the chapter because I do not think it is a viable option for many people. I also didn't want Medicaid to set the tone for this complicated discussion. I count more than twenty different factors to consider regarding long-term care. Medicaid is only one of them, albeit a big one.

Historically, and in recent memory, our seniors were cared for by family and friends. But in recent times, more and more family members have had to enter the workforce. And until recently, people didn't live as long and senior citizens were a smaller portion of the population. But more than 70 percent of us alive today will need LTC at some point in our lives. The costs for that LTC are borne by patients, Medicaid, insurance companies, and, to a limited extent, Medicare.

The cost of nursing home care has grown steadily for some time now. In 2021, the costs ranged from $2,600 to $4,200 per month. Some quotes were as high as $12,000 per month! The costs of care are increasing between 5 and 10 percent per year! A six to nine-month stay could cause a significant reduction in your savings and investments. The average nursing home stay is 2.5 years. By 2030 (seven years from now) the annual costs for nursing home care may be over $180,000, almost $15,000 a month, more than $500 per day.

If and when you need long-term care, Medicare only covers the first one hundred days in a nursing home or long-term care facility. During the second eighty days of this period, the patient is responsible for co-payments, and not all Medicare supplement policies (Medigap) will cover those co-pays.

Because our life savings will be at risk it makes sense to buy a long-term care insurance policy to help us with LTC costs. The question is which LTC policies are best for our situation—A traditional policy? A "combination" policy where LTC is included with a life insurance policy? Or one combined with an annuity?

Today, only about fifteen insurance companies provide LTC policies, down from one hundred a few years ago. The traditional stand-alone, older policies are straightforward. You pay premiums for coverage and like automobile insurance, there is no cash value. Your premiums are based on your age, health, and the amount of daily benefit (insurance proceeds) you contract for. Because of the rise in nursing facility LTC care expenses, the few companies that sell traditional policies frequently raise premiums.

Alternatives to the traditional policies include LTC coverage with a life insurance policy (with accelerated death benefits) or LTC coverage with an annuity contract. You might say you are letting the insurance company use your money for a period of time, and if LTC costs don't wipe out your life insurance benefit or the annuity investment balance, you or your heirs will receive the balance of the value of the life insurance policy, or a portion of what you invested in the annuity.

As one example, a life insurance company might offer a *combination* policy, which allows you to spread your premium payments over ten years. So a fifty-five-year-old might pay $10,000 for ten years ($100,000) and get a monthly long-term-care benefit of $5,500 for up to six years ($396,000). If he didn't need long-term care, before passing away, his heirs might receive a $130,000 death benefit. Or he could cash in the policy in later years and get back 80 percent of his premiums, $80,000, or use it like an annuity for lifetime income (your age and health may affect the payment in projected illustrations).

An annuity might have LTC coverage added with a lump sum payment used to purchase the annuity. The payout on the annuity depends upon the type and terms provided. If LTC is not needed, you could use the annuity for lifetime income or withdraw your original lump sum payment (plus interest).

An annuity may be 'deferred' or an 'Immediate', single premium annuity. Two pools of money are created: one for long term care expenses, and another for any purpose you choose. Because of inflation, the payments for LTC on this type of annuity may not be adequate. If the LTC pool of money is not used, it may be passed on to your heirs, or you could receive a stream of payments for your life or over a specified period of time. This option is available regardless of any health conditions. Women would receive a smaller payment because they have longer life expectancies than men.

Life insurance policies may offer LTC coverage as a rider. The rider will apply up to a certain percentage of the face of the policy (the death benefit). A policy might pay out up to 50 percent of the death benefit for LTC costs. The payments for nursing home care might be higher than the amounts paid for home care. Many new plans couple long-term care with whole life insurance policies.

The type of LTC plan options chosen affects the premium cost: a monthly plan option is more costly than a 'daily' option but is more flexible. With a monthly plan, you can access up to your maximum monthly amount. With a daily plan, if you exceed your daily amount, you will have a co-pay for the excess over your daily maximum.

You can choose a full "cost of care" plan or "co-payment" plan. The full cost-of-care plan is more expensive, and you have fewer, if any, out-of-pocket costs. The co-payment plan will have lower premiums.

The amount of insurance benefit chosen should be determined by how much you can contribute to your cost of care in the future. The more your projected budget in retirement will allow you to contribute toward the anticipated cost of care, the lower you can choose as your benefit amount, and the lower your monthly premiums will be. But this "self-insurance" with a co-payment could be more costly in the long run.

Generally, if the daily costs exceed the daily benefit, payments will be based upon a maximum benefit *per week* allowance. So the work shifts of an informal caregiver (who charges less) could be staggered with a formal (more expensive) caregiver so the total weekly costs do not exceed your maximum weekly benefit.

Optional Riders (for additional premium costs are): (1) dual waiver of premium (where when one spouse receives care, premiums are waived for both spouses); (2) Shared Care (that can be with one pool of money, two pools of money, or for a family with three or more members); (3) Restoration of Benefits (in case all the original benefits are used up); (4)

Return of Premium; and (5) Survivorship Benefit (where if one spouse passes, the other spouse will no longer have a premium payment).

An inflation provision in a LTC policy helps you deal with rising costs. Inflation factor options are *Simple* or *Compound*. The Compound option will result in a higher benefit (with a higher premium). Popular options are a *Simple* rate for inflation at 3 percent or a *Compound* rate at 3 percent. The Compound rate is recommended for younger insureds.

The *maximum benefit* is important too. Your daily benefit is the amount the policy will pay daily for you. The maximum benefit will be calculated using the daily benefit, an inflation option (if chosen), and the total anticipated care time purchased. For instance, if the daily benefit amount is $200 and the maximum period of coverage chosen is three years, the maximum benefit will be $219,000 (3 times 365 times $200). With a 3 percent simple inflation option the maximum benefit would increase to $253,520. You can also choose to purchase a benefit amount that is higher than the current average cost of care (for a higher premium of course).

Premiums for the traditional, stand-alone policies currently average around $3,000 per year. When premiums are raised, they must be raised for *all* policy holders; the insurance companies can't just single out certain policy holders.

Premiums are higher for *waiver of premium* and *automatic increase* riders. There is usually no premium cost for a *benefit increase* option that allows you to purchase a higher benefit using the same rates. Most policies will be guaranteed renewable (meaning you can't be denied continued coverage if you develop a condition that makes you otherwise uninsurable). If you cannot perform one or more of the Activities of Daily Living (ADL) when you apply for insurance (bathing, eating, getting out of bed, dressing, and toileting) expect premiums to be more expensive.

Premiums may be paid semi-annually, all up front, or paid up at age 65 (no more premiums once the insured reaches 65). A *single* payment, accompanying a life insurance/LTC policy is most expensive, but you won't have to worry about premium increases later.

Health Savings Accounts (HSAs) may be a good source of funds to pay for LTC costs. Distributions from HSAs may be used to pay LTC insurance premiums or to pay LTC costs directly (and still remain tax-free distributions from the HSA).

All states require policies provide a "free look" period of thirty days. During this period, for any reason, you may return the policy for a full refund of any premiums paid.

A "Benefit Trigger" occurs when the policy holder needs substantial assistance to perform at least two Activities of Daily Living for ninety (90) days, is chronically ill, or has severe cognitive impairment (the loss of deductive or abstract reasoning).

To qualify for Medicare LTC coverage, the patient must have had seventy-two consecutive hours (three days) in a hospital and subsequently released to receive Skilled Care. Skilled care is considered around-the-clock health care provided by licensed professionals under the supervision of a licensed physician.

The "elimination period" or deductible period chosen is important (30, 60, 90, 180 days). The longer the elimination period before the policy kicks in, the more out-of-pocket costs you will have after diagnosis and treatment begin. You might say you are "self-insuring" for this period. The primary reason to choose a longer elimination period is to lower the premium costs, but with inflation costs rapidly rising for LTC costs, be careful. Unless you plan to have adequate wealth in the future, a medium or shorter elimination period would be a better choice. The elimination period usually has to be met only one time during the life of a policy (lifetime elimination).

The government, the insurance companies, and you the consumer are each trying to protect resources, each trying to limit its risk of paying for long-term care. As the consumers in the equation, it is up to you (with the help of the insurance agent) to design an insurance plan that minimizes financial risk to you.

The ideal time to buy LTC coverage is when you are in your fifties and in good health. Since LTC policies provide benefits when you cannot perform two or more Activities of Daily Living (ADL), it is best to buy the policies while you are able to do all ADL (with no assistance).

Premium rates are classified as Preferred or Standard. You could even be denied coverage by some insurance companies once you have had a medical diagnosis for conditions such as diabetes, Alzheimer's, stroke, heart condition, arthritis, HIV, or alcohol or drug abuse. Just taking drugs to *prevent* any of the above conditions may result in denial of LTC coverage.

The *type* of policy is important too: Most policies are Comprehensive, covering nursing home, assisted living, and home care. Policies are also available for Nursing Home Only and Home Care Only. Most LTC policies will cover home health care or adult day care. With the many quarantine and other restrictions experienced in nursing homes as a result of the Coronavirus pandemic, many patients prefer care at home.

There are attractive benefits with policies that cover both spouses. These policies usually provide a discount. The main benefit is coverage for both spouses when one spouse is otherwise uninsurable! Other options include waiving the premiums for a surviving spouse and accessing the other spouse's benefit maximums. A patient's spouse may exempt some joint assets from being counted when trying to qualify for Medicaid. Many living choices could lower our care costs while providing the care we need.

As we get older, we could need assistance with housekeeping, preparing meals, *bathing, eating, getting out of bed, dressing, and toileting.* The last five items are considered Activities of Daily Living, which can *trigger* LTC coverage). There are several levels of care senior citizens may need (or want) that don't involve full care in a nursing home (the most expensive care).

We might want a living environment that provides socialization, recreational activities, and transportation to shopping and doctor's appointments. We may want some assistance in our lives while still enjoying a great deal of independence. If we (with the help of our doctor and family) decide we need some assistance, we should have guidance to begin our journey before the need for care.

Your local Area Agency on Aging is a good starting place to learn what services are available in your community. They advocate for the elderly and provide educational materials and referrals. They may have information on one or more of the following types of facilities: a Continuing Care Retirement Community, an Assisted Living Facility, a Board and Care Home, or an Adult Day Center. Each has features that address some of our living needs while allowing us some independence.

Besides care provided in nursing homes, LTC care may be provided for medical conditions at home or an optional living facility. We may want to address our long-term living choices sometime before our long-term care insurance policy is triggered. Care can also include personal services needed because of age, chronic illness, or disability.

A Continuing Care Retirement Community (CCRC) provides independent housing and options for every level of care depending upon your needs. You may contract for custodial care or skilled nursing if required. Your living unit usually requires an advance payment of $100,000 or more, plus monthly fees.

An Assisted Living Facility (ALF) provides support services, such as meals, housekeeping, and laundry. Most facilities have apartment-like units. You can enjoy socializing and transportation to local events. Health Aides are available to help with Activities of Daily Living, and nurses are available on a limited basis.

Board and Care Homes (BCH) provide meals, housekeeping, social activities, and transportation. Nursing services are *not* provided. Assistance with bathing and dressing can be provided at extra costs. State licensing may be required depending upon the number of residents. Some board and care homes may call themselves community-based residential care or adult foster care facilities, but there have been instances of non-compliance with city fire codes and complaints about sanitary conditions. So each facility should be carefully evaluated on its own merits and not just the care it is registered to provide.

Adult Day Centers (ADC) allow seniors to socialize, enjoy meals, and participate in educational activities during a typical workweek. These centers can provide a needed break for busy caregivers. Many guests will receive assistance with Activities of Daily Living. Some centers may be intergenerational, allowing interaction and exchange between seniors and those of younger generations. A daily fee of fifty dollars or more is usually charged.

When LTC is needed, a good step would be to hire a Care Manager, preferably one who is a member of the Aging Life Care Association. Your primary care physician, nurse, clinic, or Area on Aging can refer you to Care Managers. The Care Manager will meet with you and family members to assess your health care needs, financial options, and develop a care plan. A Care Manager and care plan are desired and sometimes *required* by the LTC policy.

The Care Manager is the team leader, the quarterback who outlines the roles of the individuals and organizations involved in the care plan. Care Managers are in the best position to minimize care costs and delay the need for the most expensive care. After a care plan has been designed, the role of the Care Manager may be taken over by a willing family member or other able individual.

If a person with life insurance is terminally ill, with less than two years of life expectancy, viatical settlements may be available. The viatical company takes over premium payments and becomes the beneficiary on the policy. The percentage of death benefit paid to the insured depends upon the length of life expectancy (from 50% if over two years, to 80% if six months or less). Proceeds from the settlement are used to pay LTC costs. Only about 50% of viatical settlements are approved.

Life Settlement options are available too. Men over 70 and women over 74 may sell their life insurance policy for its present value. However, there will be no death benefit for heirs and the distribution may be taxed.

The Veteran's Administration will provide nursing home care to veterans for service-connected conditions. The VA will also provide care for veterans who are totally disabled or rated *70 percent* or more for service-connected disabilities. For those who don't meet the criteria for LTC coverage from the VA or who have maxed out their Medicare coverage, looking to Medicaid to provide all of their LTC can be challenging. Yet Medicaid is the option that many people hope will pay for their care.

Medicaid: Long-term care was not envisioned as a significant cost to Medicaid when the program began. It was first designed for people who were blind, elderly, or disabled. Also covered were pregnant women and families receiving public assistance.

If one wants to look to Medicaid to pay for all their long-term care today, their *liquid* assets (cash, stocks, bonds, etc.) would have to be less than $2,000 to fully qualify. Some people have the bad idea of giving their assets to their children or moving them into an irrevocable trust with their children as beneficiaries. But Medicaid and most states have a "look back" period of five years, and any transfers within that time frame would still be counted as assets for purposes of qualifying for care. Check with your state to determine the look- back period for your state.

Another big concern is the risk that the children (the beneficiaries who now have the title to the assets) would make irresponsible decisions like trashing your personal residence or losing title to it. You could potentially be homeless or destitute if an irresponsible beneficiary didn't take care of the property as hoped. That said, your primary residence is usually exempt from Medicaid countable assets if you plan to return to live in it. Your car, burial policy, and business assets are usually exempt from Medicaid counting as well.

A so-called "Penalty Period" is the postponement of when Medicaid will pick up costs if your personal assets were improperly transferred. Let's say $40,000 was transferred during the sixty-month look back period (five years) before your care began, and the monthly cost of care was $4,000. There would be a delay of ten months before Medicaid would begin paying for costs ($40,000 divided by $4,000 = 10). These are not the only concerns with relying on Medicaid.

After a patient receiving LTC Medicaid passes away, states must freeze and go after estate assets because of federal law. States must go after transferred assets, exempted assets, and trusts created to qualify for Medicaid. These Estate Recovery Programs have been successful for many states.

There is also a federal law against "Medicaid Planning"—planning to qualify for Medicaid by disposing of assets. There are fines and penalties for financial advisors who participate in this type of planning. Even many attorneys are not up to date on all of the requirements for Medicaid.

Another concern is that private pay facilities close to your family may not have openings for Medicaid patients. Suppose the only facility accepting Medicaid patients is far away and not convenient for your family to visit! A better alternative is to get a LTC policy and then *you* can decide where you would like to go for care and where a TV, telephone, and other amenities are *standard* with care.

Through their Medicaid programs, many states have entered into 'Partnership Programs' with insurance companies to reduce Medicaid costs. In a *qualified state long-term care insurance partnership*, for every dollar of LTC coverage purchased, the state will exclude one dollar of your assets in qualifying for Medicaid. If your policy had a maximum benefit of $80,000 and you exhausted your full LTC benefit for your care, you could then keep up to $80,000 of your liquid assets (cash and investments) and Medicaid should pay any additional costs of care. Some states even offer protection of *all* of your assets if you purchase the state's so-called *Set Amount* of LTC insurance.

The federal government has set up *reciprocity* standards, that require states to participate in partnership programs allowing an insured of one state to have the same protections in other participating states. Not all states participate in partnership programs, so you should consider the portability of a partnership program with your current state to any future state you plan to live in.

Premiums on LTC policies are tax-deductible on a sliding scale depending upon your age (older insureds may get to deduct a higher amount). But claiming the premium may not reduce your federal taxes unless you itemize deductions and your medical expenses are extremely high—more than 10 percent of your adjusted gross income (AGI). Some states may allow a deduction for medical expenses even if you don't itemize deductions on the federal return.

Most LTC policies are tax qualified, meaning the policies meet certain IRS guidelines. Benefits paid under a tax-qualified policy are generally not taxable unless they exceed the cost of care. Neither the IRS nor Congress has addressed whether benefits paid under a non-tax-qualified policy would be taxed. If it is determined that those benefits are taxable, we should be able to deduct the medical expenses involved in the costs of care. Many employers today are offering *group* LTC policies. Employees are attracted to the benefit and the business gets to deduct the cost of premiums paid.

In summary, planning for long-term care is complicated. The biggest choice is between a traditional policy or coverage that is coupled with a life insurance policy or annuity (where you have life insurance or an investment involved). The life insurance policies or annuities with LTC coverage should be compared and analyzed for what would be best for your situation. Have the insurance agent run different illustrations with different amounts of daily and maximum benefits (time periods) of coverage. Be sure the illustrations include inflation options—especially if you are younger— age sixty or less. The more time that passes between the time of purchase and the time you use the benefit, the more inflation will have increased the costs of care.

Consider if your state has a partnership program with a *Set Amount* of LTC coverage that protects your assets. It should meet your desired level of LTC coverage and allow you eligibility for Medicaid coverage if and when required.

After you have looked at your budget and considered your preferred options, it's probably worth contacting an insurance agent who is a long-term care specialist. They can help you make a decision by running illustrations that allow you to make comparisons.

Lyn Rowe Insurance, Inc. Talk directly with Lyn: (877) 270-3127. lyn@lynroweinsurance.com/ https://www.iwantmyltc.net/

Genworth: 888.436.9678 https://www.genworth.com/products/care-funding/long-term-care-insurance.html

John Hancock: 800-377-7311
https://www.johnhancockinsurance.com/my-policy/long-term-care.html

Brighthouse Financial: (800) 638-5000 (life insurance with a long-term care option)
SmartCare Long Term Care | Life Insurance | Brighthouse Financial

Disability insurance:
Disability insurance is just as important as life insurance. We are more likely to become disabled than to die unexpectedly. Disability insurance is especially important if you are still working and your family depends upon your income. It's a good idea to have coverage to at least age sixty-five when you become eligible for Medicare. Some policies end at age sixty-five. This insurance may not be as expensive as you may think. The premiums depend upon the type and amount of coverage.

Some companies include:

Northwestern Mutual
AFLAC
State Farm

CHAPTER 8

Investing: The Road to a Better Future

If your income is low or moderate, you need to invest in stock mutual funds more than others who have already gained some measure of financial independence. The stock market and real estate markets have been the most reliable contributors to wealth. Let's get right into what I have seen work and real-life. These are practices and ideas from respected advisors and investors. When I talk about stocks and bonds, I could be thinking of individual stocks and bonds or stock and bond *mutual* funds. Most investment theories regarding individual stock or bond behavior hold true for the behavior of stock or bond mutual funds too.

A mutual fund is a collection of several stocks or bonds. One of the primary benefits of mutual funds is the fact that owning several stocks or bonds result in less risks than owning individual stocks or bonds. An S&P 500 Index fund is a mutual fund. You could say owning this fund gives you a piece of the top 500 U.S. companies. Just as a mutual fund is a compilation of stocks and bonds, a *portfolio* is a collection of mutual funds, but a portfolio may include individual stocks and bonds as well. The goal of an astute investor is a diversified portfolio.

Different investments produce different rates of returns (profits). Therefore, diversifying our investments increases our probability of earning better rates of return (and reducing our probability of loss). In most years, stocks have performed better than bonds, but there have been periods when the opposite has happened. The S&P 500 Index fund includes the 500 U.S. companies with the largest capitalization (that is the most stocks issued at the highest prices). Small company stocks (small cap) have a higher performance, but they also have more risks. Investments in stocks and real estate provide the best protections against inflation.

Between 1926 and 2010, inflation averaged 3 percent. Building a nest egg is the right idea, but your investments need to earn more than 3 percent so the purchasing power of your nest egg beats inflation. Between 1980 and 1999, interest rates paid to *fixed* income investors on bonds, CDs, and savings accounts were at least *twice* the inflation rate, but interest rates paid to *fixed* income investors have gone down tremendously. So having your money in interest-bearing bond funds or savings accounts will not adequately address inflation. Recent interest rates have been lower than the inflation rate.

Inflation had been less than the average of 3% for the past 15 years or so, then in 2021 and 2022 we got a wake-up call with inflation jumping to 8% (the highest rate in decades). Because the Bureau of Labor Statistics (BLS) now averages selected categories of expenses in the Consumer Price Index, it is difficult to know the true rate of inflation. Since banks are paying two percent or less on savings accounts, it would be prudent to include both stock and bond mutual funds in your portfolio. You can't just save as they did in the old days; you have to *invest*.

But investing is a word with broad meaning. It implies making a sacrifice today to gain something of greater value in the future. How much greater the investment will become depends upon three things: how long the investment has time to grow, how risky the investment is, and the expected rate of return (that is the profit from interest, dividends, and capital gain, the growth between the purchase price and the selling price).

The longer your time horizon for the investment, the higher the probability of greater returns and the lower the risks you will have to take. The shorter the time horizon of the investment, the more risk you would need to take to get a similar rate of return. Or you could take less risk in a shorter time horizon and expect a lower rate of return.

Those are the three cards dealt to us—time, risk, and rates of return! Those constraints are not negotiable, not subject to our will or feelings. But if you play those cards well, you are likely to succeed. What about luck, you might ask? Well, bad luck can be as probable as good luck. So it is better to just play your hand well and not make rash choices. People might suggest that they can manipulate the markets, time, and space, just don't let them try it with your money.

If your goal is to earn 20 percent on your investments, your expectations are too high. Looking for a 20 percent rate of return is close to gambling. If you are looking for a 5–10 percent return on investment, this book can help you accomplish that. Anything higher than 11 percent would simply be good luck. You can take good luck and, with strategy, lock in higher-than-average returns. You could do that by selling some winning stocks that had above average rates of return and moving the profits to less risky investments (like bonds or CDs). Think of it as being cautious or not being greedy. Think of it as good strategy.

Understand the difference between investing and gambling. Investing is taking calculated risks to earn predictable rates of return. The risks and expected returns are based on current and historical information. But gambling is simply betting that a *random* event will occur (i.e., the number thirty in black will come up on the roulette wheel). Gambling is simply relying on luck. If you are gambling, you will probably lose. The casino stays in business with the dependable 5–10 percent rate of return it gets from the table games and slot machines.

Operating the casino is an investment for the House because the slot machines are programmed to pay out only 90–95 percent of customer *plays* (and they constantly monitor the percentage net winnings and recalibrate the machines if necessary). So the House can depend upon receiving a 5 to 10-percent rate of return because of statistical probability and machine programming. The odds against an individual patron winning are high. On the other hand, if we left the casino and developed a sensible investment strategy, we could probably earn a reasonable rate of return on our money. Don't be afraid to invest; be afraid to gamble.

Two concepts help to develop a good perspective about risk: fear and greed. Imagine them at the opposite ends of the spectrum. You can't beat inflation if all your money is in safe government securities (too much fear). But neither should you risk dealing in uncovered stock *options* that require you to deliver stocks in the future, at unknown prices (too much greed). Being at either end of the spectrum would not be good. There is a lot of middle ground between the two.

A good practice is to identify our *tolerance* for risk. We could use a scale from one to ten, with ten being most tolerant and one being most risk-averse (fearful). These measurements should help our brains line up with our circumstances. You see just because someone's house is paid for, has a sizable nest egg, and a decent pension does not automatically mean they will have a high tolerance for risk. Our attitudes toward money and the unknown can have some impact on our tolerance.

And just because someone is underemployed, behind on bills, and has large obligations coming due soon does not mean that person will be risk averse (a one or two on the scale). I think he *should* be risk-averse, but psychology and attitudes come into play. As long as we are not coming from a mindset at either end of the greed/fear spectrum, we are likely to make better investment decisions. Don't be too greedy, and don't be too afraid. Don't be overconfident, and don't be too squeamish. Establishing the goals of the investment might help us establish our risk tolerance:

1.   What is the purpose of the investment? Retirement, education, car, a wedding?
2.   When do you plan on drawing money from the investment? Five, ten, fifteen, twenty years?
3.   What rate of return are you looking for? 5 percent, 8 percent, 11 percent?
4.   How much can you stand to lose on the investment?
5.   Do you want the investment's earnings to be taxed now or during retirement? and
6.   Which is more important—a higher rate of return or the safety of the investment?

The answers to the questions above should influence your risk tolerance—and probably more important, the selection of your investments. If the purpose of the investment is retirement or education, be sure to review those chapters of the book in addition to the discussion below.

What is the purpose of the investment? The purpose may be a down payment on a home, car, college education, retirement, etc. The purpose will be associated with a time horizon. And the time horizon may bring some constraints. There are great risks in purchasing stocks when you have less than a five-year time period. A balanced fund in a brokerage account would be an aggressive but reasonable choice if you have five years or less, but most advisors would say go with bonds, CDs, or a fixed annuity, especially if you are risk-averse.

Whether you choose balanced funds, stocks, or bond funds, a "brokerage" account with a mutual fund company would be good for mid-term, five to fifteen-year investments. Brokerage accounts are **not** generally used for retirement, although they could be a good resource at any age). A brokerage account is *not* tied to retirement (it's not an IRA, SEP, deferred compensation, or profit-sharing plan). Because they are not associated with retirement and deferral of taxes there are fewer conditions (strings) on their purchase or sale. Plus, if you take a distribution (a sale, withdrawal) more than a year after purchase, any gain would be taxed as *long-term* capital gains. Long-term capital gains tax rates are usually lower than taxes on wages or retirement plan withdrawals.

Just understand that brokerage accounts do not postpone taxation like 401ks, Traditional IRAs, and other retirement accounts. But they can still be a good choice for long-term investing (*especially* if you might need to take withdrawals before age 59 & ½). That's because they are not subject to the 10-percent early withdrawal tax penalty. If you are no longer working but want to invest, the brokerage account is one of your best options.

Another benefit of a brokerage account is it gives you the opportunity to buy good stocks or stock mutual funds when the stock market is down, as in the summer of 2022. Unlike the provisions with a retirement plan, you can take your money out when you want to. So you would only have to wait until the market recovers to take some profits, you don't have to wait until age 59 & 1/2. This frees you from dealing with the many constraints of IRA accounts.

With brokerage accounts you don't have to worry about whether you earned at least the amount you want to contribute to an IRA (up to $6,000 or $7,000 currently). Nor do you have to worry whether you earned too much for the type of IRA you want to contribute to.

With brokerage accounts, if you have some mutual funds or other investments that are proven losers, you might decide to sell them to offset expected capital gains that will be taxed. The maximum capital loss you can deduct against your other earnings like salaries is $3,000 per year. If your net loss is greater than $3,000 the additional loss can be carried forward to future tax years.

Long-term capital gains tax rates are not high to begin with. So selling the losers should be primarily an investment decision, not a tax-saving decision. If you can avoid paying high commission charges on your investments, you would have a head start towards profitable investing.

Commissions can average 5 percent of your investment, and you may not even get good advice for such a fee! A *no-load* mutual fund company does not charge a commission for purchases (or sales) of investments. There are several no-load mutual fund companies in existence today—Vanguard, T. Rowe Price, Fidelity, Janus, to name a few. Some socially conscious mutual funds might also not charge commissions. No-load mutual fund companies will provide limited financial guidance on their websites, by telephone, or by chat. But if you make all of your initial transactions online, you will lose the benefit of their input.

Even no-load broker/dealer companies have departments that will prepare a portfolio of investments and manage the portfolio for you (for additional fees). But if you understand the concepts and strategies discussed in this book, you shouldn't need those services. The time period you are investing for is an important factor in the decision of what to invest in.

Time Period: If your plan is to let the investment grow for five years or longer, you may want to purchase stock (equity) mutual funds. If your time horizon is less than five years, you might want to invest in CDs, bonds, or savings accounts. A *balanced* fund is a nice compromise because they contain both stocks and bonds.

Many people could have benefited from the *75-percent* growth in the stock market from 2007–2019. If one's primary source of income was to be social security and a small pension, he or she would have greatly benefited by investing in stocks during that period. If time is on your side, don't be afraid of stock market fluctuations. Be sure you have enough in savings, bonds, or other resources to wait the market out (it could take five years until stock prices bounce back but it has usually taken less time).

Bonds are safer for shorter-term investments but investing in bonds is more complex in times of low-interest rates. Investing in government bonds has always been a safe, community-minded gesture, but they have limited benefit to people who have low incomes. Government bonds may have been okay a few decades ago when the interest rates bonds paid were higher. You only have to go back to early 2021, interest rates were at historic lows. Towards the end of 2022 rates on commercial, corporate bonds were becoming more attractive.

When interest rates rise, the value of bonds (previously issued) will go down. New bond buyers will want the higher coupon interest rates paid on the newer bond issues. At a minimum, you want your investments to earn more than 3 percent (the average inflation rate). If you want bonds to preserve your investment principal and earn some interest, short-term or intermediate-term bond funds would be best. Long term bonds have not been paying the highest interest rates as they did historically. If you like government bonds, TIPS may be an acceptable choice (Treasury Inflation Protected Securities). But I think folks whose income is low would do better with commercial bond funds. Folks who are in the 25% or higher tax bracket could benefit from government bonds.

Government Securities come in two categories: federal notes and bonds, and the so -called *municipal bonds* which are state and local government bonds. Both types of government securities pay less interest than commercial bonds issued by corporations. Government bonds are often recommended for higher-income taxpayers since they might benefit from tax savings. Municipal bonds (state and local) are exempt from *federal* income taxes, and federal bonds and notes are exempt from *state* income taxes. Municipal bonds from *your* state of residence may even qualify for exemption from both federal *and* state income taxes.

This is probably a good time to say that no investment can guarantee prosperity. And most investments have some risk (although federal government bonds are considered risk-free). In most cases, the higher the expected rate of return on an investment, the higher the risk. When risk is extremely high, be careful you have not crossed over into gambling. Buying a particular stock mutual fund (or stock) with a history of earning 8% is investing. It is investing because they are traditional investments in a regulated market, and its history is an indication of what it can potentially earn in the future (8 percent). Any venture without a reliable track record is a gamble. Let's be blunt. The shiny object that is supposed to make someone rich with very little effort is designed to appeal to their greed. It's probably another version of "drop the pigeon" or "the Spanish handkerchief." Walk away as fast as you can.

People in different walks of life have grown fortunes through luck, hard work, or some combination of the two. Because one has achieved success with one's professional pursuit (acting, ministering, music, or playing sports) does not mean investing with them will result in financial success for you. Often, when someone achieves success, "handlers" come around to help them grow and maintain their fortunes. Don't let handlers or someone's celebrity status be the motivation for you to invest with them. Do your homework on the venture and have someone else check *your* work before you invest.

The rate of return you are looking for should determine how aggressive you need to be. But don't expect to earn more than 10 or 11 percent in the stock market, even though earning more is possible. The more earnings you *need*, the more aggressive you should be, but you shouldn't plan on earning more than 11 percent per year on average. Some years the market may have negative movement (down 10%). In other years it could move up 20 percent.

I once had a client with a laid back lifestyle and a good pension from his previous employer, so earning 5–7 percent was an adequate target as a rate of return on his investments. We estimated his target rate of return based upon the following:

1. The amount he was investing was enough to generate a fair amount of interest, dividend, and capital gain income over the years;
2. He planned to only take moderate withdrawals (he had a simple lifestyle and a public pension from the government; and
3. With only a 5 percent projected rate of return, less his expect withdrawals, we projected him to have as much in the account after twenty years as he had when we were designing his portfolio to begin with!

The bottom line is he only needed a 5-percent rate of return to maintain his principal after allowing for his withdrawals. So why build a portfolio with an average expected return of 11 percent (all stocks) with the added risk? By choosing large company stock funds like the S&P 500 and a good number of bond funds (about 50 percent of his portfolio) we were able to lower his portfolio's risk–the standard deviation or volatility. The trade-off was a lower expected average rate of return of between 5 and 7 percent.

When the tech bubble burst with the market crash of 2000–2002 and everyone was moaning over the lower values of their investments, he called and asked how his investments were doing. I said your stocks are down about 10 percent. But since you have a good number of bond mutual funds in your portfolio, the interest income you have received puts your holdings back to about where they were when you started. So the bonds gave him safety and income, and the stocks still provided a lot of upside, growth potential. My client was happy. The balance in his portfolio was stable. The stock funds in his portfolio then grew exponentially after 2002, and he left a sizable legacy to his family.

Not many moderate-income investors will have sizeable savings, plus have steady income from defined benefit pension plans. So if you need to earn a 10 percent rate of return on your investments, you should be more aggressive and have more than 50% of your portfolio in stock mutual funds. But it may take longer than five years to realize that 10%. Because of the volatility of having mostly stock funds, it could take ten years, or it could happen in three! Be prepared to ride the market out, if and when it is down along the way.

Being unnecessarily aggressive can bring unnecessary worry. My wealthy tax client, a doctor married to a scientist, was not served well by one of the big Wall Street advisors, the ones who take 5 percent of your investment in fees. She complained to me that her portfolio had gone down significantly when the tech bubble burst. I thought to myself, "Why would an advisor design such an aggressive portfolio for a couple that brings home over a million dollars a year?" Maybe he got higher commissions from selling those particular aggressive growth mutual funds? (That was a possibility!) Maybe the advisor wanted to impress them by choosing funds that had exceeded the stock market average? If so, shouldn't he have known better? Shouldn't he have known you don't chase "hot" funds? Shouldn't he have considered that with his clients' wealth, they didn't need to take on those unnecessary risks? I kept my mouth shut and completed their tax returns.

Back to risk tolerance: Other questions an advisor should ask are, "How would you feel if your investment went down 10 percent?" And more importantly, what would you *do* if your investment went down by 10 percent? Our feelings can affect our behavior. If we were to make a detrimental move because of a reduction in price, we could make matters worse. We could make a temporary reduction a permanent loss. Think of your tolerance for risk. Don't succumb to an unrealistic fear.

Shouldn't our fear be in line with the impact of the loss of the principal on our current (and future) financial situation? As we invest, we always want to have enough in an emergency fund to cover three to six months of expenses (to pay for rent, utilities, food, etc.) So we will want sufficient amounts of cash, savings, and CDs to give us some short-term comfort as we invest our other money long-term.

Our long-term investments need to grow to adequately meet our long-term goals and future needs. If the value of your invested principal went down 5–10 percent, and it would not significantly affect your ability to meet current and long-term obligations, and you have several years before you need to touch the money, your tolerance for risk *should* be high. You are in a position to shoot for an 11-percent rate of return if that is what you think you need to achieve your financial goals. Again, if losing 5–10 percent on your investment will not prevent you from meeting your immediate and future needs, your risk tolerance should be *high*.

If you do **not** have enough in cash, savings, CDs, and bonds to meet four to six months of your current monthly expenses, your risk tolerance should be *low*. Try not to let your investing put you into a situation where you need to borrow or take money out of your long-term investments prematurely. If the market is down and you take your money out, you lose. And if the money was in a retirement account, Uncle Sam will hit you with a 10-percent tax penalty for early withdrawal—that will add to the loss!

I can only share how I think about how you *should* feel if your investments fell in value (with the knowledge the stock market should come back within a few years). But I will not be there with you if your investment loses value. It's best to decide ahead of time whether you can be okay waiting as long as four to five years for your investments to recover. If you don't think you could wait it out, you should be a little more conservative. Just don't be so conservative that you don't plan to overcome the impact of inflation and income taxes. That's especially important if you are going to need a healthy rate of return (7 percent or more) to accomplish your long-term goals.

Taxation: Do you want the earnings from investments to be taxed now, in the future, or not taxed at all? Balance is a good perspective to have on taxes. You don't want to ignore potential taxes, but we shouldn't be obsessed with trying to avoid them altogether either. By investing in municipal bonds, your earnings could come out tax-free! Roth IRAs could also result in tax-free earnings if the money is left at least five years and you are at least 59 & 1/2 when you take the earnings out.

A *brokerage* account, mentioned above (a non-retirement investment vehicle) could result in lower taxes because of *long-term capital gains tax rates of* **0**, 15, or 20 percent, depending upon your tax bracket. The long-term capital gains tax rate (LTCG) will apply to investments you hold for more than one year. In 2021, if your taxable income was less than $40,000, the long-term capital gains tax rate on the gain from your investments would have been **0 percent**; if your taxable income was between $40,001 and $441,000, the LTCG tax rate was only **15 percent**; and for taxable income above $441,000 the LTCG, tax rate was **20 percent**. *Qualified* dividends are also taxed at the long-term capital gains rate. So many dividends received can result in lower taxes for all income brackets.

As shown above, the effective tax rates on *brokerage* accounts can be much less than the "ordinary" tax rates on salaries, Traditional IRAs, and other sources of income. Although LTCG tax rates on mutual funds inside of brokerage accounts are lower by comparison, you do have to pay taxes in the year that income is credited to your account. (That is the interest, dividends, and capital gains). So taxes are *not* deferred on brokerage account earnings as they are for traditional IRAs, 401Ks, retirement plans, and deferred compensation plans. The year when you actually sell the investment will result in LTCG tax on the difference between your purchase price (i.e. the cost basis) and the proceeds from the sale (assuming you held it for one year or more).

Reducing taxes for the current year: If you are interested in reducing your taxes in the current year, you can contribute to a deferred compensation plan, a traditional IRA, profit-sharing plan, 401K, 403B, or Self-Employment Plan (SEP). Your contribution will lower your gross income for the year, and taxes will be *deferred* on the earnings on those investments until you make withdrawals sometime in the future. This can make sense if you are in the 25 percent or higher tax bracket or you need additional money now. When withdrawals are made from these plans, they are generally taxed at the "ordinary" tax rate (often higher than the tax rates for LTCG). If it is the case that you don't need money now and will be in a higher bracket in retirement, a Roth IRA would be a good choice. (You can continue to maintain the 401Ks and deferred compensation accounts in addition to the Roth).

If you don't *need* the tax savings now, using a Roth contribution will give you tax free earnings from the investments during retirement. Be sure you qualify to contribute to either type of IRA you choose. Qualifying is based on your income level and whether you or your spouse had a retirement plan available at work. The allowable income limits for Roth IRAs are usually higher than for a Traditional IRA. The thresholds increase every year. See the limits at https://www.irs.gov/. Remember, there is usually a 10 percent penalty for withdrawals made from IRA accounts before age 59 & 1/2.

Tax Free Income? Besides the Roth IRA, there is potential for tax-free income with life insurance products. But that can be confusing if the policy is not simply "term" insurance that pays a death benefit to your beneficiaries upon your death. Because "permanent" insurance policies can be so complicated and confusing, I don't recommend them for people with low or moderate incomes—especially if their goal is saving taxes! If your income is low, why not focus on earning money? Make enough money to live well and pay taxes on it.

With permanent insurance policies, one of the biggest risks is taking money out before age 59 & ½. You would not only be taxed on the withdrawal but will likely have to pay a 10-percent penalty! You can also expect a stiff service charge for early surrenders of those policies within the first few years of ownership. I think insurance policies should be chosen for insurance needs, cash value and income tax reduction should be secondary considerations (The book has a chapter on insurance).

What to invest in? After considering all of the above, we can now concentrate on our portfolio of investments and which mutual funds will best help us achieve our goals. Individual stocks might be an option for a brokerage account, but since it is hard to predict the future of individual stocks, I don't recommend relying too much on them in building your nest egg for retirement. A rule of thumb on buying individual stocks is to limit them to 5 to 10 percent of your total investments. That is a good rule for any risky, speculative investment. If stocks like Apple or Amazon now represent a significant part of your portfolio, as you get closer to retirement you might want to gradually diversify into some other Fortune 500 Company stocks, large cap stock mutual funds, and corporate bonds. (Remember what happened to Enron's stock!) The same advice applies if you are currently in retirement.

In 2020, there were nearly 1,000 mutual fund companies and 10,000 mutual funds. Worldwide, there are about 80,000 mutual funds! So where do you begin? We begin with no-load mutual fund companies. Different no-load companies will emphasize different strategies and different mutual funds. Vanguard has the largest variety of funds and largest amount of money managed. They invented the mutual fund, but most of their funds have a $3,000 minimum (except for funds within IRAs, which might be lower, with $1,000 minimums). Fidelity is known for good research tools and has similar terms. Don't forget Janus, T. Rowe Price, and others who may have lower minimums to begin investing.

To build a good and diversified portfolio you have to determine which mutual fund companies have the type of mutual funds you want and their minimum investment requirements. Consider that a fund you like at Vanguard might be closed to new investors, but there is a similar one available at Janus with similar stocks and fund objectives. T. Rowe Price and Vanguard might have a similar fund that you like, but Vanguard's minimum entry amount is higher. Think of it like grocery shopping. You know what you will need to prepare a great dinner. But you may have to stop at two or three stores to get the best versions of the foods you want so you can prepare the best meal.

Diversifying your investment portfolio is thought to be the best way to minimize risk and earn a good rate of return. It's another way of saying "don't put all your eggs in one basket." There are several ways to diversify, but too many mutual funds can defeat your purpose if you duplicate the same stocks (or bonds). For instance, a large cap mutual fund may have many of the same stocks as the S&P 500 Index fund (they both may have a lot of shares of Apple, Microsoft, and Amazon stocks). So owning both doesn't give you much diversification.

Michael Falk, certified financial analyst with Focus Consulting Group, recommends only two to five mutual funds. I like as many as fifteen if they are diversified well (not too much individual stock duplication). Mr. Falk suggests that our behavior in investing is more important than the investments we choose. He recommends that we set a time once a year to reassess our investments. If we have a strategy pre-planned of what we would do the following year if our stock investments went up and what we would do if they went down, we could take the emotions out of our future actions.

In other words, if our investments go up at least 15 percent, we plan to take some profits (sell) and buy some bonds. Or if our investments go *down* by 10 percent, we will buy more of those stocks or at least *not* sell any of our stocks until they have rebounded. Having made our plans ahead of time, we just need to follow them.

But following our plans can be challenging with so many experts on the TV, radio, and internet telling us what to do and trying to explain why the stock market is doing what it is doing. With so much noise, it is tempting to make a move you did not plan on. If you remember, what *you* were going to do (your plan) if the market did X or Y, you will make a better decision. One thing I learned in the Air Force is almost anyone can fly a plane, but it is more important that you learn how to land one!

I think some expert commentators watch what the stock markets are doing and *then* look for explanations. Their analyses make it sound like the market will respond the same way if a similar external event occurs in the future. But correlation and causation are two different things. Back in the 1980s, some said if the NFC won the Superbowl the stock market would go up, and if the AFC won the market would go down! Ha! That was about as scientific as flipping a coin! The best analogy I have heard is that the stock market behaves like a teenager. No one can explain why they do what they do! One day they make the Principal's Honor Role. The next day they bring home a drop-out and asks can they spend the night! Any day the kid comes home with his or her brain intact is a good day!

As long as the market goes up 11 percent per year on average, there is no need to try and figure out why it's up or down day to day or month to month. Plus, if your investment portfolio is well diversified, much of the analysis doesn't matter anyway.

One final point: If your goal is to maximize your earnings, be careful of chasing the hottest stock mutual funds. Most funds will return to the mean average of the market (11 percent). So if you buy a fund after it's gained 20 percent for each of the past two years, watch out! If you like the fund for reasons other than its recent earnings like it meets your goal of diversification, take a look at how it performed over the past five and ten years. The objective is to verify that the fund has a stable earnings record, not to verify that it can consistently outperform the market. Few, if any, mutual funds have outperformed the market average of 11 percent for more than ten years running. If its ten-year average shows it has had a good earnings rate, it is likely a well-managed mutual fund.

Options to diversify your portfolio include having some portions of:

1. Index Funds
2. Managed Funds, including Growth, Income, & Value funds
3. International Funds
4. Sector Funds (like Energy, Technology, Financials, Health Care, etc.)
5. Real Estate (Real Estate Investment Trusts—REITS)
6. Bond Funds (corporate bonds, government bonds)
7. Balanced Funds (they will have some stocks, some bonds, and maybe some target date funds)
8. Tax-Managed Funds (they try to have fewer taxable transactions, probably not good in a retirement account **or** for people with low to moderate incomes) and
9. Cryptocurrency (maybe 1–2 percent of your portfolio—otherwise, I do not recommend).

The following discussion should also help you in designing a well-diversified portfolio.

A *prospectus* explains the goals and investment strategies of a particular mutual fund. The broker/dealer mutual fund company may also give brief descriptions of the goals of their different mutual funds in their *family of funds*.

A simple way to invest in the stock market and avoid management fees is choosing an **S&P 500 Index fund** and the **Russell 2000 Index fund**. The S&P 500 Index measures the stock values of the largest 500 U.S. companies. The Russell 2000 Index measures the stock values of the bottom 2,000 of the 3,000 smaller capitalized U.S. companies. Index funds are simple; if the average prices of the stocks of companies included in the index went up 10 percent, the value of your investment in that index fund also increases by 10 percent.

Fees on index funds are low because the funds are not actively managed. Your return on investment is basically the average rates of returns of the stocks of the companies included in the index. But the market does go down at times, and that's when *actively* managed funds *might* perform a little better than index funds. So I like having both index and managed funds. (That also helps achieve diversification).

In choosing **actively managed** mutual funds, you should consider the goals of the fund. If you want *income*, mutual funds with stocks of companies that consistently pay dividends would be a good match. Corporate bonds paying interest would also provide a steady source of *income* (although bonds provide safety, bonds usually won't provide much growth in price over the long-term). See bond funds below.

Stock mutual funds that emphasize dividend income might be great if you are older and would like to live on the income or you just like consistent income. There are also so-called *growth* mutual funds. These funds consist of companies that don't pay much in dividends but focus instead on the growth of their stock prices. In the 1990s, Microsoft paid very few dividends, but people still bought Microsoft because its price grew consistently. To try to make all investors happy, some mutual funds emphasize both growth *and* income! But before you make a decision, look at their performance (rates of return) over five and ten years. Just because the goals of the fund check off a couple of desirable boxes doesn't mean the fund is performing well.

Some mutual funds focus on value. With **value funds,** the fund managers look for companies whose stock prices they believe are under-priced. The idea is there might be a lot of upside price growth potential for those stocks.

Another way to diversify your investments is to include **sector** funds. These mutual funds consist of companies within certain industrial sectors (like health care, energy, pharmaceuticals, real estate, technology, etc.).

Real Estate Investment Trusts (REITs). REITs allow you to invest in real estate through the ownership of mutual funds. Some REITs may focus on commercial properties, and some on residential properties. There are also REIT index funds where your earnings depend upon the average growth of the real estate market represented by that index. REITs provide some diversity from the major stock markets. Some believe the correlation between the stock-market behavior and the real-estate market varies between 60 and 80 percent. Others say there is no diversification (or 100% correlation), but I think 60–80 percent correlation is about right.

Since the stock market and real estate are the largest sources of wealth for the average investor, having a REIT in your portfolio allows you growth opportunities and diversification as well. REITs are required to pay out 90 percent of their profits to investors each year. I like a portfolio to include about 15 to 20 percent in REITs.

Another important addition to a portfolio is **international funds.** They will give you an ownership interest in foreign companies. If and when stock prices of American companies are down or "flat," foreign company stock prices may not be as negatively impacted. An international fund is different than a *global* fund because global funds can have a lot of American compa-nies included (remember, you are buying the international fund to diversify *from* US companies). Like the REIT above, an international fund provides diversification and an opportunity for growth. Just know that international funds are considered riskier than the U.S. 500 Index fund. An inclusion of 10–15 percent in a portfolio should be good.

Bond funds will help to reduce the risk (the standard deviation or volatility) in your portfolio. Because bonds generally have a lower expected rate of return than stocks, your overall rate of return on the portfolio will probably go down as well. Unless you want to be very aggressive (looking for a rate of return of 10 percent or higher), including some bond funds in your portfolio of investments is a good idea. If you are going to be aggressive with your traditional IRAs by being heavy in stock mutual funds, you still should have some bond funds to withdraw your required minimum distributions (RMD), in the case the stock market happens to be down all year.

As mentioned before, as interest rates go up, the value of bonds you currently own will go down, affecting your total rate of return. Prior to 2021 and 2022, interest rates were at historic lows. Therefore, the only direction interest rates could go was up! Solution: Purchase an *intermediate* term bond fund (five to ten years to maturity). By the Fall of 2022, interest rates had risen a bit. Bonds are always a good source for steady interest income. They also give you some stability for times when the stock market goes down with a "correction" or even in the remote possibility of a market crash.

Government bonds can be federal, state, county, or local. If safety is your primary concern, government bonds are the way to go, but unless you are in a higher tax bracket (25–33 percent or above), corporate bonds with higher interest rates may be a better choice. Corporate bonds are pretty safe too. And if you are buying bond *mutual funds*, even if one company in the fund went under, that won't have much effect on the whole bond fund.

The lower interest rates paid on government bonds are accepted because the income is generally exempt from taxation. State or local bonds (called municipal bonds) are exempt from *federal* taxes. Conversely, interest on federal bonds and notes are usually not taxed on *state* income tax returns. Government bonds are **not** recommended for traditional IRA or traditional 401K accounts since distributions from those retirement accounts are fully taxable. As such, there is no tax benefit with a *traditional* retirement account for accepting their lower rates of return (But I would not rule them out for inclusion in a *Roth* retirement account if one's income is high *and* safety was their primary goal). The percentage of bonds typically included in a portfolio has often been associated with one's age.

What proportion of stocks versus bonds should one have? One *crude* rule of thumb is to subtract your age from one hundred, and that will tell you the percentage of stocks. So a forty-two year-old would have 58 percent of his or her investment in stocks or stock mutual funds (one hundred minus forty-two equals fifty-eight). The rest would be in bond funds (42 percent). But rules of thumb fail to consider that we don't all have the same needs, risk-tolerances, or goals.

If you understand the discussion so far, you should be able to tailor the mix of your portfolio to address your specific investment goals. You will have an emergency fund to handle three to six months of spending needs. You would add to that enough in bond funds to ride the market out up to five years if necessary. You would know how to respond when the market goes up or goes down and not violate the strategy of buying low and selling high.

With the risk that interest rates may go up a bit more in the future (it is now 2022), it would be good to lean more toward stock funds for growth but do buy some bond funds to provide safety and interest income. The chapter on retirement will discuss strategies to optimize your rates of return while providing a cushion for your cash needs.

Balanced funds are mutual funds that include both stocks and bonds. If the forty-two year old above found a balanced fund that had 58-percent stocks and 42-percent bonds, that would give him the equivalence of the rule of thumb theory and his job would be finished—for the time being. He will be 42 for only one year and the fund will not "re-balance" as he ages (to replace stocks with bonds). To address this concern, many mutual fund companies have come up with life cycle or target date funds.

Life cycle or target date funds attempt to mirror the proportion of stocks to bonds that one should have for safety based on his or her age. For instance, in 2022, a target date fund titled L2050 (almost thirty years from now) might have 65-percent stocks and 35-percent bonds. Then each year as we approach 2050, the fund managers will re-balance the fund in line with the remaining years to 2050. So in 2025, the fund might have 55 percent in stocks and 45 percent in bonds. By 2050, the fund might have 75-percent bonds and only 25-percent stocks. The assumption is that you will mostly want safety because you will be retired and will begin drawing money out in 2050.

The thing to remember about target date funds is to pick one based upon *when you expect to start taking money out* and <u>not</u> one that corresponds with the age at which you intend to retire. You can avoid the 10% penalty for early withdrawals from a retirement account after age 59 & 1/2. So although you might be 59 & ½ in 2040, you might choose the 2050 fund if you wanted to be more aggressive or did not plan on taking any money out until 2050. Target date funds are great if you do not want to make the effort of re-balancing and adding bonds to your portfolio in the future. But if the target-date fund re-balances during years when the market is down (to buy more bonds), that can negatively impact the fund's total rate of return. If you want to be more aggressive, want a higher rate of return, and still have some safety, a *balanced* fund would be a better choice.

Tax-managed funds are for investors who want growth in a *brokerage* account but do not want to pay much tax on their earnings (good for those in the 25 percent or higher tax brackets). A tax-managed fund manager looks for companies that don't pay out a lot of dividends or interest. The mutual fund manager also won't do a lot of trading, which can result in capital gains flowing through to owners of the mutual fund. Tax-managed mutual funds are not appropriate in a retirement account or deferred compensation plan because retirement accounts are not taxed until the money is taken out anyway. Like its cousin, tax-exempt government bonds, tax-managed mutual funds are not appropriate for those in the low or middle-income brackets because they may sacrifice income in their efforts to avoid taxes.

Cryptocurrency (crypto): It is hard to know what to make of cryptocurrency. If it doesn't make sense to you and you can't afford to lose the investment, don't invest in it. If you can afford to lose the investment, limit it to one (1) to two (2) percent of your investments. There is a chapter on crypto that goes deeper into it, but the recommendations don't change.

Besides being extremely volatile in price, there are complaints about high transaction costs. Crypto can also be difficult to trade. The President of the U.S. is requesting input from some 20 federal agencies by October 2022 in efforts to regulate crypto. But volatility, value, and negotiability are my main concerns.

If you had bought Bitcoin in 2013 you might have been sitting pretty (for a while). The value of Bitcoin rose 300% in 2020. But by July 2022 It was down about 70% from its all-time high. In fact, by July 2022 all of the top ten crypto currencies had seen steep declines, the steepest declines were in the most expensive ones. There are many negative concerns about cryptocurrencies such as alleged violations of anti-laundering laws and efforts to avoid investor protections.

But some people like cryptocurrency because they are not well-regulated (or as crypto proponents like to say—they are *self*-regulated). That feature might be a natural attraction for radicals and non-conformists, anti-establishment, and anti-banking industry proponents. Promoters of these alternative currencies are relying on our dislike of traditional systems, but we need to weigh the negative aspects of cryptocurrency as well as their potential for profit. We need to focus on the investment characteristics of cryptocurrencies and not just see them as opportunities for political statements (stiffing the man).

On the positive side there are reports of digital currency being used by major players in several markets. Because of the proliferation of cryptocurrencies, innovative entrepreneurs are finding ways to employ them in their business models. But there are concerns of how to value these investments and the potential impact of federal regulations coming on the horizon. There is much more discussion in the chapter on cryptocurrency.

Building a Portfolio of Investments: Now that we have discussed most of the players, how do you use them to build a diversified and balanced investment portfolio appropriate for you? There are many places to look for guidance and many options for diversification. Before we dive into the mechanics, there are a few questions to ask yourself: How close are you to when you will need income from the investments? How *long* will you need the income? Are you going to make one withdrawal or a stream of withdrawals over five, ten, fifteen years, or over your lifetime? What rate of return are you looking for—5 percent, 8 percent, 10 percent? And how much risk or volatility are you willing to accept? (Adding intermediate term bonds will reduce the risk and volatility of a portfolio). Are you a socially conscious investor? It's best to answer these questions before you begin to look at particular mutual funds.

Many no-load mutual fund companies have a 'walk through' process (for free) to guide you in selection of mutual funds to achieve your goals. The walk-through process can be good if you are planning to have most of your investments with one mutual fund company and you feel that company has asked you appropriate questions during the walk through process.

You could also develop your own portfolio if you are comfortable with investment concepts. A third option would be to accept their recommendations from the walk-through and add a couple of mutual funds that you think will broaden out the portfolio. For instance, you could add a REIT or an International fund if they did not already recommend them in their walk-through process. There should be no cost to use the mutual fund company's walk-through process.

Whichever route you take, the longer you can let your investments grow, the better your chance of earning greater returns. The less you need to earn from the investments, the less risk you will need to take and the less aggressive you will need to be.

Remember, bonds help reduce risk. So consider how much (what percentage) of your portfolio will need to be in bonds (or bond funds) to address your risk tolerance. If your portfolio includes both retirement accounts and brokerage accounts you should decide what percentage of your investments you want in each. Remember that brokerage accounts will be taxed currently.

With both your retirement and brokerage accounts , you will need to consider what proportion of stocks versus bonds you would like. With your retirement accounts, remember that tax-free bonds and tax-managed stock mutual funds are not appropriate. If you have fifteen to twenty years before you will be taking withdrawals, you might want 60 – 80% in stock mutual funds—especially if volatility, ups and downs, don't bother you. (During the last five years you could re-balance by adding more bonds to reduce the portfolio's volatility and give you more safety).

Depending upon your investment goals, you might have more of your investments in your retirement accounts to reduce your current taxes. Just remember not to be so overweighted in the retirement accounts that you have to touch them before age 59 & ½. Both your retirement accounts and your brokerage accounts should be diversified. Ideally you will not have the same mutual funds in your retirement accounts as you have in the brokerage accounts. That can be challenging and that is why I am open to as many as 15 mutual funds in your total portfolio. But the more mutual funds you have, the more you have to watch out for stock duplication.

Diversifying a portfolio on a limited budget can be challenging if the minimum initial investment per mutual fund is $2,500 to $3,000. But Vanguard, Fidelity, T. Rowe Price, and others have lower investment minimums for IRA accounts and Target Date funds when they are included in IRA accounts. The minimum is usually only $1,000 in the case of retirement accounts.

Target Date funds are rated as moderate risk because they include bonds, but you could be looking at only 5–8 percent rates of return, even with the funds with longer future "maturity" target dates. If those rates of return are within your investment goals, you should be good for a few years. Except I don't believe a fund with75% bonds and 25% stocks is appropriate for most people and that's the proportion of bonds versus stocks at the maturity of most Target Date funds. The companies may have available other funds for $1,000 minimums besides Target Date (Life Cycle) funds. Vanguard's Star fund comes to mind (a balanced fund). It can be purchased in either an IRA or a brokerage account.

Fidelity, Janus, and T. Rowe Price have lowered their minimums to entry, but that could change. That flexibility is important when you are looking for a brokerage, non-retirement account. Some no-load mutual fund companies will even allow you to purchase a fund if you allow a monthly draft from your bank account (fifty dollars or even twenty-five dollars a month in some cases). So even on a tight budget you can and should invest. You may have to make a few phone calls or visit the no-load mutual fund company's web sites for answers.

Vanguard's Star fund (a balanced fund) has a $1,000 minimum investment and balanced funds may be a better choice if you desire a higher rate of return than Target Date funds. The Star fund is about 60-percent stocks and 40-percent bonds, and unlike the target date (life cycle funds), rebalancing (selling stocks to buy bonds) is not performed based upon dates, that in effect, may reduce future earnings.

You have control over the composition of your portfolio. Others may provide guidance for what they believe is a "good" portfolio. In a perfect world, accountants who understand business and financial statements would be in a good position to estimate the value of a company and its stock price. But the world is not perfect, and accountants are not better at guessing stock prices than the general population. With managed mutual funds , a fund manager is deciding which stocks (or bonds) to invest in. They do this full-time and are better at it than the average investor.

If you create a portfolio with 25–30 percent index funds and the rest in "managed" funds, you will have the best of both worlds. You can ride the wave to the top with index funds as the stock market reaches new highs while paying low fees. And in times when the market is not doing well, your managed funds (large company, REIT, international, health care, or sector funds) may not drop as sharply. I believe seven to ten mutual funds (a combination of stock funds and bond funds) can provide good diversification.

At this time, you can expect an 11-percent rate of return on stock mutual funds and approximately a 4-percent rate of return on bond mutual funds. If you bought both stock funds and bond funds, your rate of return would be the weighted average or average of the returns on the two sets of funds. So if your portfolio operates with 75-percent stocks and 25-percent bonds, your expected rate of return after a period of time would be **9.25**

percent ([.75 times .11] + [.25 times .04]). Portfolios should be re-balanced occasionally to keep the desired ratios of stocks to bonds. Once a year should be frequent enough.

If your stock mutual funds performed as expected and increased in value by 11 percent while your bonds were only earning 4 percent, after a couple of years your stock funds may represent a larger proportion of your total portfolio. So if you wished your ratio of stocks to bonds to come back into the balance of 75:25, you would need to sell a portion of your stock funds and buy more bonds to return to the 75:25 ratio of stocks to bonds (a re-balance). Yet you will not want to sell stocks when the stock market is down (or your particular stock mutual funds are down). That's because you would be selling the stocks at discounted prices to buy the bonds. Remember, almost anyone can fly a plane, but you have to know how to land one.

It's best to execute your first mutual fund purchases with the assistance of the mutual fund company's customer service representative. It takes time to get familiar with the company's funds, accounts, and online platforms. Even if you have the correct understanding of what you are trying to do, the company's online platforms may have quirks or ambiguous descriptions of mutual funds or transactions. You might think you have purchased a mutual fund, but all you've done is open a sweep account and expressed an interest in a particular fund. Months could go by before you realize the oversight.

Opening a money market or FDIC-insured "sweep" account with a mutual fund company without assistance may be okay. These are similar to cash accounts used to fund your investments. But when you want to purchase a stock or bond mutual fund (where risks are involved), it is better to have a company representative walk you through the transaction. Any lack of communication could cost you.

The representative will also be able to discuss your investment objectives and strategies and offer suggestions. Investing is not something you need to do in a hurry. After you gather information and decide upon a strategy, sleep on it if necessary and call the company the next day. But if a representative suggests something they can't explain to your satisfaction or you disagree with, get a second opinion from another representative before moving forward.

Many of us received good advice from our parents or other older mentors decades ago. But some of the old advice will not be good today in our current interest rate and high inflation rate environment. Putting the money under the mattress was helpful and thoughtful decades ago but inflation today would cut the purchasing power of those dollars sharply. Not putting all your eggs in one basket is still good advice.

"Don't owe anybody a thing" might have been good advice when new cars cost $2,000 and a nice house cost $12,000. In the 1960s, many state universities even had free tuition. Today, with the great necessity of borrowing, getting low-interest rates may be the only options we have for large purchases. It might be helpful to reflect on a few mistakes I have seen people make because they did not get good advice:

1. Invested $5,000 in an IRA, even though he didn't have $5,000 in wages that year (you must have *wages* or *self-employment income* of at least the amount you want to invest in an IRA).

2. Panicked and took $155,000 out of his portfolio of stock mutual funds two weeks after making the investment because the investment's value dropped about $15,000 (the tech bubble burst). Of course, the market came back within a few months, but the $15,000 loss was permanent because he had sold and gotten out. I blame the advisor for not educating the client about the volatility of the market and not appreciating his low tolerance for risk.

3. While still working, took $100,000 out of an IRA prior to age 59 & 1/2 to pay a mortgage off early. He got hit with a 10-percent penalty for early withdrawal. Plus the $100,000 withdrawal pushed him into a higher tax bracket! He paid almost $40,000 in income taxes and penalties on the $100,000 premature distribution! His mortgage interest rate was only 3.5 percent, which was not considered high at the time. But he just didn't want to owe anything

on his house! *It would have been much better to leave the money in the stock market for another few years to grow another $25,000 until he was 59 & ½. During retirement he would have had less taxable income, putting him into a lower tax bracket. He could have then taken out about $80,000 of the appreciated money to pay off the balance of the house note and still had a substantial amount of his investment in place. The 11 percent average earnings in the stock market were a lot higher than the 3.5-percent interest rate he was paying on the mortgage (which by the way, was tax-deductible). So his effective interest rate on the note was really only about 3%!*

4. For nearly twenty years she consistently invested in government bonds through a deferred compensation plan, because a co-worker told her *bonds were safe!* Her average earnings were only 4 or 5 per-cent over those years. After you subtract 20 percent for taxes, her net return was only about 3–4 percent. Inflation averages 3 per-cent, so there was less than a 1-percent increase in her purchasing power! During that same time period, the stock market averaged 10 percent per year. *Bonds should not outweigh stocks in your invest-ment portfolio unless you are already retired or planning on drawing from your portfolio <u>and</u> you want some safety from market volatility!*

5. He put significant money into a startup business venture without a business plan. He only made about $5,000 over a three year period while having three times as much in business expenses. *A business is not a hobby. If you don't have solid prospects for income, control your expenses on a start-up business.*

6. He didn't pay income taxes on retirement income because a lawyer told him that taxes were unconstitutional and he had already paid taxes on his pension income. After all, they told him, taxes had been withheld from his salary! *Some* of our retirement income may not be taxable, but pension fund managers are pretty good at reporting the taxable portion of our retirement income correctly. You can't ignore the taxable income reported on a form W-2P which is also reported to the IRS. You can challenge it in writing

if you think it is wrong but you can't ignore it. After the government put Al Capone in jail for tax evasion, we should have learned it is a good idea to respect the tax laws.

7. Finally, be careful investing with banks. Most people think of banks as *safe* places to put money. But commercial banks were not allowed to sell mutual funds to the general public prior to the de-regulation of the 1990s. So many of their advisors are not experienced in investing in stock mutual funds. Although cash deposits are guaranteed by the FDIC, our stock or bond investments are *not* insured like our checking, savings accounts, and certificates of deposit. Since they generally charge 5 percent of your investment for commissions, you would be paying a high price for the illusion of safety. And banks have been known to hedge their bets against the very investments they recommend to their clients. If the market goes up, they make money. If the market goes down, they make money (Nice work if you can get it).

Comparison of Different Investments and Inflation Over Time

Ibbotson® SBBI®

Stocks, Bonds, Bills, and Inflation 1926–2019

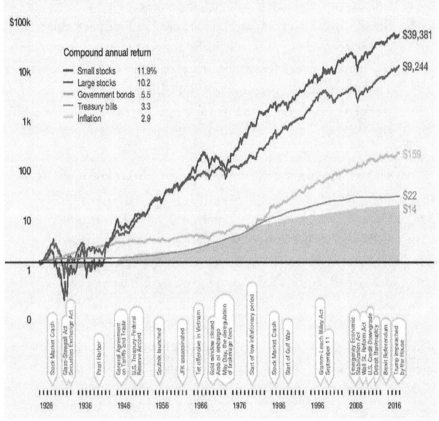

Past performance is no guarantee of future results.

Hypothetical value of $1 invested at the beginning of 1926. Assumes reinvestment of income and no transaction costs or taxes

This is for illustrative purposes only and not indicative of any investment. An investment cannot be made directly into an index.

© 2020 Morningstar, Inc. All rights reserved.

There are several points to take away from the nearly one-hundred-year Ibbotson chart (12).

You should decide which points are most important for you. The chart shows the growth of a $1,000 investment from 1926 to 2019.

1. The rate of return on stocks is about double the rate of return on government bonds;
2. Inflation averaged approximately 3 percent;
3. Small cap (small company) stocks are the best performers and out-performed large-cap stocks by almost two percentage points (1.7 percent more). Remember, they are more volatile.
4. The less than two-percentage point difference between the two stock classes amounted to $30,137 more growth over time ($39,381 less $9,244).

We see the significant drop with the stock market crash of 1929. In response to other major economic events, there were also dips in 1974, 1987, 2001, and 2007, but the market always came back! Yes, there was a crash in 1987, but it is hardly a bump in the long scheme of things. My good friend was heart-broken that he did not sell his company's stock prior to 1987. Since he had recently left the company, he felt compelled to sell the stock (and just take the loss). If he had just held on to the stock, it bounced back within a year! I wish I had been smart enough to tell him to hold on to it, but I was young and had not learned yet about stock-market behavior. Buying a home is also a significant investment. That chapter is next.

CHAPTER 9
Home Buying

The two most reliable creators of wealth in the United States have been the stock market and real estate. Owning a business, receiving an inheritance, or insurance proceeds may also result in wealth, but they are more complicated and less predictable. This chapter seeks to make the purchase of a home a more pleasant and profitable experience.

Buying a home may be a good investment, but an investment should not be our primary motivation. Investment means different things to different people. A home should be purchased primarily for enjoyment. Even if you don't plan to live in the home the rest of your life, it is a big commitment and should be a place you expect to enjoy for at least a few years. Keep in mind that if you live in the home at least five years, you may be able to exclude up to $250,000 of *gain* from the sale of the home, $500,000 if married filing jointly (that is tax-free income!). So enjoying the home for a minimum of five years can be very profitable.

You might also enjoy tax deductions for mortgage interest expense and property taxes—if itemized deductions return to their previous place in tax planning. The current high *standard* deductions are temporary and set to expire in 2025. Connected to the currently high standard deduction is the $10,000 ceiling on state and local tax deductions. That ceiling for now negatively impacts individuals in states with high property taxes. If and when these two provisions expire or are overturned, your tax deductions for interest and property taxes may again become higher than the standard deductions. (When a portion of the home is used as a business, you should be able to take tax deductions for a portion of the mortgage interest expense, property taxes, insurance, utility costs, repairs, and depreciation on Form 8829 regardless of the standard deduction or limitations mentioned).

If you are a Veteran entitled to a VA Home Loan, you can borrow up to $647,200 in 2022. The amount may be over $970,000 for high cost areas. VA loans are a great way to buy a home if you don't have at least 20% down and would be required to pay as much as 1% of the loan balance for mortgage insurance. But if you have good credit and can afford at least 20% down, you might get a better interest rate with a conventional mortgage.

Whichever route you take for the loan, there are several steps you can take in the process of planning to buy a home. Working with a good real estate agent can save you some of the steps, but you should still perform any calculations you can so you will be comfortable with the mortgage payment. Since the seller ordinarily pays the real estate agent, their fees should not be a big concern (there may also be real estate agents in your area who will work for buyers or work as dual agents if you want more independence in the agent).

Because the traditional agent works for the home seller, you need to be sure to protect your interests in the deal. The best way to do that is to have detailed questions about any property before signing a contract (or offer). Even though the real estate agent may work for the seller, they are required to be honest with you. That is why your questions are so important. To properly prepare for the home purchase, perform as many of the steps below as you can.

1. Look up the current thirty-year mortgage rates (i.e., 4.25 or 4.5 percent). Use Google or ask your credit union.
2. Consider what price range might result in a comfortable mortgage payment for you.
3. Visit a mortgage calculator (i.e., Lending Tree or your credit union) to calculate an estimated mortgage payment based on your estimated price range and the current interest rate.

4. Speak to an insurance agent about the estimated monthly homeowner's insurance cost for a home in your price range.

5. Speak to a local real estate agent or visit your county's website to get an estimate of property taxes for a home with your expected home value (or selling price).

6. Prepare a monthly household budget that includes the total estimated mortgage payment (principal, interest, insurance, and property taxes). Include any fixing-up costs in your budget

7. Consider how much you might qualify to borrow. Usually, lenders require that the mortgage principal and interest, plus payments on your other debts, not exceed **43 percent** of your income. For example, if your monthly income was $3,750, and your other monthly debt payments amounted to $850, the most your *principal* and *interest* payment could be is about $750; (850 plus $750) divided by $3,750 = 42.66 percent (just under 43 percent). Depending on your credit score, the lender may allow the debt to income ratio to go higher than 43 percent. This 43% threshold could change depending upon economic conditions.

8. Once you are comfortable with your estimated monthly payments, speak with a real estate agent or a trusted lender to see about getting pre-qualified for the *maximum* amount you would consider borrowing (remember your budget from above).

9. Create a checklist of what you desire and require in a home. Maybe you don't want to be closer than fifteen miles to an airport or you want to be at least two blocks away from a busy street. What is the maximum distance you want to live from work? How will you get to work or other activities? Are there certain industries you don't want to be close to? Is there a concern about air quality or noise pollution? Make a checklist and share it with the real estate agent. That will save you time and energy in finding the house you will like.

10. What other local features or conditions should you know about?

11. How would you feel about a homeowner's association? How much will the homeowner's association fee be (there are pros and cons with homeowner's associations. Some can be nice; others are a bit hard to work with).

12. Learn from the real estate agent the seller's motivations for selling. Depending upon the seller's circumstances, the seller may be more inclined to accept your reasonable offer. Remember, the seller has their asking price, but the real estate agent is required to submit any reasonable offers to the seller.

13. Ask the real estate agent whether there are any local incentives to help borrowers (first-time or other) to help with down payments (there may even be some federal government money or city, state, or county money to help you get into a home).

14. Inquire of the real estate agent who will be performing the home inspection. Obtain a copy of the home inspection checklist then have a friend assist you in inspecting the home to double-check the findings or other conditions that concern you. **Be sure any repairs or changes you request get written into the contract/ offer.** Verbal agreements carry <u>no</u> weight in real estate transactions.

15. Be careful not to pay more than you should for the home. If the price is right but the interest rate is high, you can likely refinance in the future with a lower interest rate.

16. Remember that mortgage insurance is usually required if you owe more than 80 percent of the property's value. Mortgage insurance is of no benefit to you, so you want to avoid it if possible (once you have paid the mortgage down to less than 80 percent of the home's value, be sure to contact the mortgage company to make sure they stop billing you for it). A VA loan could be a viable option to avoid mortgage insurance.

17. Finally, although you may want the numbers to work to get into a home, you may have to live there longer than you planned to. So make sure the home will be one you will like. After you have settled on a nice place to stay, it's time to invest in an automobile. But

first things first. We don't want to tie up our funds or credit up with an expensive car before finding a nice place to live.

CHAPTER 10

Car Buying

B uying a car can have a significant impact on our cash, our credit, our patience, and all three. Maybe leasing a car has become popular since there is less haggling over price. But leasing can often be a time bomb ready to go off at the end of the term of the lease. Either buying or leasing a car can be a trying experience if you don't like to assert yourself with strange salespersons. Not everyone is equipped to engage in argument. Salespeople are trained to be assertive and overcome objections so our work is cut out for us.

We can prepare for these transactions and negotiate terms we find favorable, or we can agonize for several years over what we could have or should have done when we had the opportunity. I imagine you have decided to be prepared and to negotiate. This chapter is designed to help you with both.

Whether you decide to lease or purchase there are some basics to follow. If you are going to purchase, the price of the car and the interest rate are the big concerns (and let's not forget the reliability of the vehicle you are interested in). If you lease, something I call the implied interest will then be a concern.

I used to have a handle on buying cars. I would just buy used cars, one to five years old because new cars lost a lot of their resale value as soon as we drove them off the lot. I would offer the dealer 35% less than the asking price by offering to pay in cash and let them talk me up to paying 25% less for the car.

If I financed any part of the purchase, I would have pre-arranged credit through my credit union. I would pay about a 25% down and sign a note for three or four years. The shorter payoff periods resulted in lower interest rates, resulting in less total interest paid.

Then the virus and pandemic hit (2020-2021) and there was a shortage of used cars. With the economics of supply and demand, a shorter supply of used cars meant higher prices. In 2021 I heard used car prices increased as much as 20%, and I don't think it makes sense to pay a premium for a used car. A smart young NCO in the Air Force suggested that buying a brand new car at a discounted made more sense than paying a premium for buying a used one. With the rebates and other options the dealer could use, a new car could be a better deal. And the bigger dealerships had more freedom to reduce the price.

Only in recent years, have friends and clients told me of car leases that resulted in favorable balloon payments at the end of the leases (that's your opportunity to buy the car). If you want to buy the car at the end of the lease, you need only to arrange financing with a good interest rate. But with most leases I had personally observed, the lessee was upside down at the end of the lease (the value of the car was less than the amount they would have to pay to buy it). So leases were not my cup of tea.

That introduces the concept I call 'implied interest'. Let's say you have a lease requiring payments of $6,000 per year for five years for a total of $30,000. And let's say that same lease requires a balloon payment of $15,000 at the end, if you would like to then purchase the car. If the best historical information you have (Blue Book history, Consumer Reports Magazine, etc.) allows you to project that this particular make and model automobile will be worth only $10,000 after five years, then you would be upside down by $5,000. ($15,000 less $10,000). This $5,000 is what I called *implied* interest. I called it implied because interest is not discussed in the lease agreement.

On the other hand, if your research on this particular vehicle shows that the vehicle would probably be worth $17,000 in five years, then you would not be upside down, in fact you would be $2,000 in the black by buying the car ($17,000 less the $15,000 purchase price).

Your knowledge of a particular make and model, the quality of your research, and the terms of the lease inform whether a particular lease will be favorable or not. And there is still some risk because the car may not work out as well as previous models did historically. One of my friends got a favorable lease on an Audi. Of course he didn't know it was favorable until the end of the lease. But if someone else had leased that same make and model Audi from a different dealer with different terms, the outcome might have been different.

The terms of the lease matter. The amount of the monthly payments, our estimated rate of depreciation, and the amount of the balloon payment will determine whether the lease will put us upside down or in a favorable position at the end of the lease. It will be up to us to do diligent research on the projected future value of the vehicle (how well we estimated its rate of obsolescence—its rate of depreciation). Some cars lose their market value faster than others, that happens whether you are leasing or buying.

If you decide to buy a brand-new car, the larger dealerships have more options to make deals with you. You might even be able to negotiate down the price by having dealerships compete with their offers. Yes, tell one dealer the price and terms another one offered and give them a chance to make a better offer. Keep in mind the Inflation Protection Act of 2022 may provide a $7,500 credit for the purchase of a new electric vehicle and a $4,000 credit for the purchase of a used electric vehicle.

Remember to pre-arrange financing with your credit union so you can depend on being charged a fair interest rate. If the settled upon price meets with your satisfaction and the dealer wants to run a credit check to offer you a lower interest rate than the credit union, that may be okay. Having a few inquiries against your credit within the same 15 to 30 day period will not significantly affect your credit score. But you don't want to have credit checks once a month for several months. Plan ahead and get the car purchased inside of two weeks of searching. Try and have all credit inquires done during that same two week period. It's probably a good idea to shore up your credit score before looking for cars if you can.

The two main factors when buying a car (as far as negotiations go) are the price and the interest rate. Most of us appreciate the concept of price but we might not appreciate the impact of a 2-3% higher interest rate. A higher interest rate also makes your monthly payments higher and you will wind up paying more for the car. Determine how much you can afford to pay per month before you speak with a salesperson.

How much you can pay per month is not something to share with your salesperson! If the salesperson consistently presses you for it, do yourself a favor and walk out. He or she will respect you more and you will not have wasted your time with someone who is not interested in negotiating in good faith. You need to be focused on getting the price and the interest rate as low as possible. Run different scenarios with different interest rates, prices, and years of payments at home and you should be able to ball-park an estimate of the monthly payment in your head as you negotiate.

It is not too difficult to estimate how much per month your payment would be. But first look at your budget or spending plan and see how much per month you can handle (without sacrificing other priorities). You can use the calculator below or any popular on-line calculator to estimate what your monthly payment will be. Run the calculator for different amounts, different numbers of years, and different interest rates before you go into the dealership. Remember the shorter the term of the note and the newer the car, the lower interest rate you should receive. Run several loan scenarios and note what you monthly payments would be. Keep this information to yourself. Once the price has been agreed upon by you and the dealer and you know your interest rate and number of months of the loan, re-run the calculation to double check the monthly amount and confirm it is within your budget. You should have a minimum of 24 hours to rescind the contract if you need to. https://www.bankrate.com/loans/loan-calculator/

Keep in mind your three objectives as you negotiate. The fact that a five year loan of $20,000 at 3% equals a monthly payment of about $360 is good to know, but your job is to get the *selling price down*, the *amount borrowed lower,* and the *interest rate down.* The fact that $360 per month is within your monthly budget is coincidental to the negotiation. Remember the scenarios you ran as you discuss different prices for different model cars with the dealer. Focus on the best deal <u>and</u> stay within your budget range. Don't forget to estimate and budget the car insurance separately. It's not included with the calculator. Your credit union or insurance agent can give you a ballpark estimate of a monthly cost based upon the model and year of car. Talk with them ahead of your negotiations.

Something else that has helped me is to limit the potential makes and models of cars you consider buying. The greater the number of models and years you consider, the more research you will have to do and that can be overwhelming. For instance, if you consider three different model cars for three years (2023, 2022, and 2021) you would need to have researched the price and other information on nine different cars (3 times 3years = 9). If you are going to consider four car models now you need to research 12 cars (4 times 3 years = 12).

If you are going to buy a used car either from the dealer or an individual, be sure to have it checked out by a qualified mechanic. This is especially true when purchasing a car from an individual. If you buy from an individual, you will likely have to sell your current car on your own and not have the opportunity for a trade in.

Do not mention you have a trade-in or negotiate trade-in issues until you have worked out all the other terms on purchasing the car. That way you can focus attention on the true value of your old car without worrying about whether you are being asked to pay more for the new car to offset the consideration given for your trade in.

When you go to look for a car is important too. The best time to look for a car is at the end of the month and in the middle of the week. At the end of the month dealers may be trying to meet their sales quota numbers and that can provide an opportunity for you. You also don't want to shop on the weekends because there may be too many other prospects looking. You want to be only one of a few potential customers, not one of many!

It's probably a good idea to enumerate the many points laid out above:

1. Purchase from the largest dealerships unless you are buying from an individual
2. Have your financing prearranged so you can focus on getting the price down
3. Have all credit inquires completed within a 30 day period to protect your credit score
4. Focus on getting the lowest price and lowest interest rates
5. Determine how much you can (and are willing to) pay per month before you go looking
6. Keep how much you can pay per month to yourself
7. Go to a financial calculator and run scenarios of monthly payments for a range of different prices, periods, and interest rates (a minimum of 9 to 12).
8. Limit the potential makes, models and age of car to three or four.
9. Shop for a car only at the end of the month and during the middle of the workweek
10. Don't mention or deal with your trade-in until you have worked out all other terms.
11. If you want a lease, do your research on the car's resale value history. Considering the lease terms and balloon payment, project whether you will be upside down at the end of the lease.
12. If you believe you will be upside down, try and negotiate down the monthly payments and the balloon payment. If the dealer is inflexible, turn down the lease. Don't dig yourself into a hole.

Planning for retirement is an even bigger project than buying a home or a car. We tackle that next.

CHAPTER 11

Retirement Planning (Your Transition to a Better Lifestyle)

Retirement means different things to different people. Some people think it should begin at the age at which you can draw your full social security benefit (age sixty-six or sixty-seven). Some people think you should retire as soon as you can; others enjoy their work too much to even think about it. Before we discuss the amount of money you will need to retire, let's discuss some other aspects of retirement.

In a country that puts such a premium on youth and technology, many people believe senior citizens can no longer contribute to the workplace. So if you have work that you enjoy, think long and hard before deciding to sit on the sidelines. It may be almost impossible to get back into the game.

Some occupations allow a full retirement pension benefit even before reaching the age you qualify for full social security benefits. So one could retire as young as thirty-eight, forty, or fifty-five with the military, police, or fire department. What we do in retirement, regardless of age, has a tremendous effect on our quality of life and longevity.

Because many young military retirees were dying in their early fifties, the Air Force came up with its Aerobics Program in the 1970s. The goal was to get Airmen accustomed to exercises that strengthened their hearts and lungs in the hope that a healthier lifestyle would give their retirees more longevity. That was of great benefit and is probably why many military retirees are still around and in good health today. Since health is always a concern, consider how you will maintain your health in retirement.

Gym memberships can be great, just remember to attend. There are probably as many reasons to retire as not to, and many are related:

Why retire?

+ You have accumulated enough money (assets) to retire comfortably
+ You don't like your job
+ You would like to participate in other activities
+ You want to travel and see the world
+ You would like to spend more time with friends and family; or
+ You have health issues.

Why not retire?

+ You have not accumulated enough money to retire comfortably (or you are not comfortable with your estimations)
+ You do like your job (you get recognition, appreciation, and find purpose in work)
+ Your interests in outside activities are limited
+ You already spend an adequate amount of time with friends and family; and
+ You have no health issues.

Don't let the simplicity of the above lead you to think that the decision to retire is simple. The decision to retire is still an individual one, and if you do, you will need to decide how you will fill your day with activities. And if you underestimate the financial resources you will need to make retirement comfortable and fulfilling, it may be very difficult to replace the earnings you give up. Your health could be the deciding factor.

There are people younger than fifty with poor health and people over seventy in great health. Some will retire without having saved enough for the lifestyle they desire. Others accumulate more than they will ever need and will continue to work. Some retirees find activities that are interesting and rewarding. Others find themselves bored and depressed. You want to have an alternative plan (a second fallback plan), not just the one you eagerly look forward to implementing.

Another question to ask is, are you really retiring, or are you just transitioning to other income-earning activities? If the latter is the case, you definitely should have more than one plan in place. This chapter can help you figure out how much money you will need to save. Just be sure that the other income-earning opportunities can be realized. If your plan is to retire without guaranteed fixed income, you need to make sure that you have considered all of your future needs and whether the expected resources (your accumulated nest egg) will be enough.

With philosophy out of the way, the goal for the rest of this chapter is to help you project how much you will need "post work" and how much you need to accumulate to make your retirement more comfortable. Let's look at the traditional financial scenarios during retirement.

The ideal retirement foundation is thought of as a three-legged stool. For example:

Defined Benefit Plan (annuity from work, sample)	$1,500
Social Security Benefits (sample)	$1,167
Personal Savings & Investments (IRAs, 401Ks, deferred comp.)	<u>$1,000</u> (monthly from your nest egg)
Total Monthly Resources	<u>$3,667</u>

The calculations in this section focus only on the *personal savings & investments*—IRAs, 401Ks, deferred compensation, and brokerage accounts (brokerage accounts are accounts outside of retirement plans, but you can still count on them as resources during retirement). With fewer and fewer employers providing defined benefit plans (lifetime annuities), it's up to workers to build up their personal savings and investments—their nest egg. *Be sure to look at the chapters on Medicare & Medigap and Long Term Care to factor those costs into your financial needs during retirement.* The chapter on investments will be of benefit too.

Re-visit chapter 2 on spending plans and budgeting. Be sure the budget for your retirement years includes medical costs, long term care, and expenses of your planned activities. Don't underestimate the expenses since creating additional income during retirement can be a great challenge. You will want to include adequate amounts for travel, recreation, and medical care. For some reason, some financial advisors believe your expenses will decrease during retirement. That may have been true thirty years ago, but I would not rely on that thinking today. It would be better to overestimate expenses and plan to save more than to do the opposite. The rest of this chapter includes challenging and detailed calculations. You may even want to take a break and come back fresh before proceeding.

These are the most difficult calculations in financial planning (and probably the most important). Imagine taking apart an automobile engine and then putting it back together! The engine is your retirement finances running smoothly. By taking the engine apart and putting it back together, we can familiarize ourselves with all its parts and how they work.

In the Air Force, we often asked, what is the mission? The mission is to calculate the monthly amount we need to save in order to enjoy the lifestyle we would like in retirement. But two other calculations are just as important as the monthly amount we will need to save. And the three calculations are not necessarily performed in the order listed:

1. Determine how much money to accumulate (the nest egg)
2. Determine how much to put aside each month or year during your accumulation phase (your working) years; and
3. Determine the monthly withdrawal (distributions) you can expect to take out during retirement.

Each of the steps require complicated calculations, but once the calculations are done and done correctly, you will not have to perform your retirement calculations again — except for a significant change in your circumstances (like marriage, loss of a spouse, inheritance, major job change, etc.).

Why are these arduous calculations necessary? Financial planning software and online calculators often ask us to make assumptions in the information asked of us, and we don't even know many of the assumptions built into the program's calculators! So we don't just have to be careful of garbage in, garbage out (GIGO). Now we have to weigh the validity of what's inside of the computer as well (the calculations and assumptions that are beyond our control, algorithms). By performing these calculations ourselves using our own formulas in a spreadsheet or financial calculator, we have more control over any assumptions being made. So for the next few paragraphs, we are going to play amateur actuaries. It may be hard and tedious, but it is only math, financial concepts, and formulas, and you can handle them all.

Because retirement involves long-term planning, the time value of money concept must be factored into the formulas. In building our nest egg, we need to consider inflation—both before and during retirement. Inflation is one reason we don't want to rely too much on bonds in our portfolio—either before or during retirement. Inflation has historically averaged 3 percent per year. The government has changed the goods included in the Consumer Price Index basket over the years, but most financial observers agree that a 3-percent average inflation rate is a good assumption (the 6 to 8 percent inflation rates experienced in 2021 and 2022 are anomalies, but our project involves several decades).

The compounding of earnings is geometric, which makes projections difficult without using financial calculators or formulas in spreadsheets. I attempted to simplify the calculations and explain financial jargon as much as possible. Each of the concepts and factors below are helpful to calculate how much you will need to save for retirement. The following includes sample numbers, but after verifying that you can make the same calculations, you should be able to substitute your own numbers. Let's begin:

1. Your current income is $32,000, and you want to replace that during retirement (higher numbers will work too)
2. The amount of *fixed* yearly income you expect from other sources (pensions). Let's say it will be zero
3. The amount of yearly social security benefits you can expect (Let's use $14,000)
4. The inflation rate you expect (Let's use 3 percent)
5. Your current age or age at which you will begin investing (let's use age thirty-five)
6. The rate of earnings (profit) on your investments pre-retirement (let's use 11 percent—all stock mutual funds)
7. The rate of earnings on your investments during retirement equals 7 percent (that's composed of 65-percent stock funds and 35-percent bond funds)
8. The age at which you expect to retire or start drawing from your nest egg (let's say age sixty-seven)
9. The age at which you expect to stop drawing (let's say age ninety); and
10. The amount of money you currently have saved (let's say zero).

As mentioned before, with online calculators, we might be forced to enter variables that don't apply or that we are not currently concerned with. For instance, income tax rates. It is easier to subtract a percentage for income taxes *after* we have a better idea of what our income will be during retirement. Or if we expect to be in the 20% income bracket, we could increase the amount of monthly income we want by 25 percent (1.25 times $32,000 = $40,000). That way, your after tax earnings would be at least 75% of your targeted income goals. But of more importance is the *future* value of our targeted income.

The following paragraph attempts to address a 20 percent tax rate during retirement using the FINRA calculator (the Financial Industry Regulatory Authority) calculator. Let's look at an example before we get to the calculations we will perform and rely on.

If we enter our $18,000 ($32,000 less $14,000 of social security) and other information into the FINRA calculator: https://tools.finra.org/ retirement_calculator/, we will be asked for our current income tax rate and expected income tax rate during retirement. If, in our example, we entered 20 percent as the current tax rate and 15 percent as the tax rate during retirement, the calculator tells us we need to save $2,262 per year (or about $190 per month). An even smaller savings amount is calculated if we show zero taxes during retirement, but we will double-check these numbers with our own calculations.

Of greater concern is the FINRA calculator assumes you will earn the same rate of return on your investments both before and during retirement (11 percent in our example). Realistically, in retirement, you will want to move some of your investments into bonds and perhaps a few CDs because they provide a safety cushion in times when the stock market is down. Because bonds pay interest rates lower than 11 percent, you may need to invest a little *more* monthly to build an adequate nest egg. That way, you could enjoy the standard of living projected while incorporating bonds into your portfolio after retiring.

The following calculations are made with a spreadsheet or handheld financial calculator. Now *we* control the assumptions.

Let's revisit what we are trying to accomplish. We want to replace the equivalent of $18,000 per year (but in tomorrow's dollars). That's how much we will need after subtracting our expected social security benefit of $14,000 from the $32,000 per year we plan to live on (you might choose a higher or lower number after learning your required monthly saving to achieve that). Per the example, at age sixty-seven, the future equivalent of $18,000 is $46,351 (that's thirty-two years ahead with 3-percent inflation).

We next need to calculate how much we will need to accumulate over the thirty-two years until retirement—while assuming we can earn 7 percent on the balance of our accumulation during twenty-three years of retirement, it's called *the present value of required capital*. You could say this step looks forward while using both historical and future variables. The result is $723,704. If the number seems large, that's because it is adjusted up for inflation. Your monthly withdrawals in retirement will seem large too.

We can use the Excel worksheet below (found at my website). We could also invest in an HP 12C (Hewlett Packard) or other handheld financial calculator that would allow us to control the input and formulas.

If we put the same variables into an HP 12C handheld calculator and save $206 per month ($2,472 per year), we would accumulate a nest egg of $724.678. That is only off by $974 from the Excel spreadsheet, spread over thirty-two years, it's probably just rounding. What's more important is to be sure we have entered the right information, the variables (Items 1–9). The detailed step-by-step keying for the calculator input are listed after the spreadsheet.

ALL of the information we enter into the calculator is important to calculate the equivalence of the $18,000 a year we want to replace until age ninety. Feel free to change any of the variables that fit your situation or expectations. Maybe you want to have higher income during retirement? Perhaps you expect to live until age ninety-five? If so, change the numbers.

The result of our calculations is the monthly amount you will need to invest during your working years to accumulate the nest egg (thirty-two working years in the example). Investing $206 per month should accomplish that goal.

The final calculation is the monthly draw (payments to you). That comes out to $3,969 per month. That might seem like a lot, but it is in tomorrow's dollars. That last calculation may help you in making comparisons to lifetime annuities offered by insurance companies (contracts that promise you income for life or a certain time period). More on the topic of annuities to follow.

The worksheet below can be found at my website: https://guilford-taxman.com/ under Services and Retirement Planning. (Estimated Retirement Needs Worksheet). After download, be sure to enter your data on the "Input" worksheet. The worksheet below is the output and shows the calculations made as a result of the variables entered into the Input worksheet. The first numbers mentioned are from your input, the second numbers mentioned are the sample numbers that were used to verify the formulas.

ESTIMATED RETIREMENT NEEDS WORKSHEET

	Your Numbers	Sample Numbers
Please enter the required **annual** information on the **Input** Page.		
Your Current Age	35	50
Retirement Age	67	66
Desired Income during Retirement	$ 32,000	$ 56,000
Expected Social Security (In Today's Dollars)	$ 14,000	$ 15,000
First Expected **Fixed** Benefits (Guard, Civil Service, Pensions, etc.)	$ -	$ 14,000
Second Expected **Fixed** Benefits (Guard, Civil Service, Pensions, etc.)	$ -	$ 21,000
Third Expected **Fixed** Benefits (Annuities, Pensions, etc.)	$ -	$ -
Expected Inflation Rate (Probably 3%)	3%	3%
Expected Investment Rate of Return Pre-Retirement (11% or less)	11.0%	9.0%
Your Life Expectancy (in years).	90	90
Calculation of Present Value of Expected Annual Needs:		
Desired Income During Retirement	$ 32,000	$ 56,000
Less Expected Fixed Income Resources:		
Expected Social Security	$ 14,000	$ 15,000
First Expected Fixed Monthly Benefit Amounts from Above	$ -	$ 14,000
Second Expected Fixed Monthly Benefit Amounts from Above	$ -	$ 21,000
Third Expected Fixed Monthly Benefit Amounts from Above	$ -	$ -
Total of Expected Fixed Income Resources	$ 14,000	$ 50,000
Expected Annual Income to Be Replaced (at Present Value)	$ 18,000	$ 6,000
Future Value of Expected Annual Income Calculation		
Present Value of Expected Annual Income	$ 18,000	$ 6,000
Inflation Rate	3%	3%
Retirement Age minus Current Age	32	16
Future Value of Expected Annual Income	$ 46,351	$ 9,628
Calculation of Present Value of Required Capital		
Future Value of Expected Annual Needs	$ 46,351	$ 9,628
Earnings Rate Post Retirement **7%** (((1+Earnings Rate)/(1+Inflation))-1)	3.88%	3.88%
Life Expectancy in Retirement Years	23	24
PV of Required Capital to Accumulate (Nest Egg)	**$723,704**	**$154,338**
Current Investment and Savings Balances on Hand	$ -	$ 50,000
Projected Future Value of Savings & Investment Balances	$ -	$ 91,985
PV of Required Capital Less Projected Future Investment	$ 723,704	$ 62,353
Monthly Investment Needed to Accumulate PV of Required Capital	**$206**	**$146**
Expected Future Monthly Payouts (Adjusted for Inflation)	**$3,969**	**$825**

We could perform the same calculations and compare the results with lifetime annuities offered by insurance companies. Some information below is repeated to work with the financial calculator.

(1) Assume you invest $206 per month for thirty-two years, and your average rate of return (profit) is 11 percent. That will yield a nest egg of about $724,678 (pretty close to the $723,704 calculated above). (2) If you use a life expectancy of twenty-three years (age ninety minus age sixty-seven), and the *balance* of your principal continues to earn 7 percent during retirement, you could make withdrawals of about $3,973 per month (or $3,969 a $4.00 difference from the spreadsheet). Note that is adjusted down to account for 3-percent inflation. An earnings rate of 7 percent during retirement adjusted for 3-percent inflation yields a net interest rate of 3.88 percent. We are halfway there.

To perform the calculations, you would enter the following numbers into a financial calculator. I like to use the HP 12C handheld calculator. They cost about seventy-five dollars, but they are a good investment. I have only needed to replace the battery once in twenty years.

When using the HP 12C calculator, the numbers are keyed *before* the functions. The first function below is "Pmt" for payment. The second function is "n" for number of years. 32 years in our example. Pressing "g" before "n" converts years into months; 384 will appear. Int. is for interest "I" on the calculator. Don't forget the "g" before pressing "I," and so on. Continue entering the numbers and functions after them (functions are bold). At the end of the first calculation, for the nest egg, press FV (for future value). At the end of the second calculation, press Pmt (for payment).

(1) **Nest egg** = $206, **Pmt**; 32, **g, n** (384 months); 11, **g, Int** (.9167 per mo.); 0, **PV**; **FV** = **$724,678.**

(2) **Monthly** withdrawals = 23, **g, n** (276 months); 3.88, **g, Int** (.32 per mo.); 0, **FV**; $724,678, **PV**; **Pmt** = **$3,973.**

Notice how the Future Value ($724,678) is used as the Present Value in the second-to-last step of the second calculation. Future Value must first be "zeroed" out in the second calculation.

Since the results using the calculator verify the calculations on the spreadsheet, we can have confidence that the spreadsheet formulas are valid. The spreadsheet has a lot of flexibility except for the earnings rate (7 percent) during retirement. In the interest of saving space, I compromised and fixed it at 7 percent (about 65-percent stocks and 35-percent bonds). Adjusted for 3-percent inflation, that comes out to be a net interest earnings income factor of *3.88 percent*. If you had more bonds and brought your average rate of return down to 5 percent, the inflation adjusted rate of return (interest factor) would be about 2 percent. You can make that change in the worksheet if you like. These challenging calculations may help you evaluate the profitability of annuities.

Most of us wonder whether the payouts on lifetime annuities give us a good rate of return on investment. You may have heard that the fees on life annuities are high, and they are. Some say that is the price you pay for guaranteed income. Remember that the numbers above are adjusted for inflation, and payouts lasts only until age ninety in our calculations. So if you purchased an annuity for $724,678 and the insurance agent's illustration pays out a monthly amount of $3,969 for *life*, (adjusted for 3% inflation) that is a good option.

But the insurance agent's illustration may not be adjusted for inflation. Using a 7 percent rate of return, **not** adjusted down for inflation, would give you payments of $5,290 per month. If the insurance illustration shows you would receive $5,290 or higher *for life*, that sounds like a good annuity contract. Be sure that there is a "period-certain with refund option" so money will go to your beneficiaries if you pass away unexpectedly. Or be sure the annuity has "straight joint life with survivor benefits" in case you are married, so your spouse will receive benefits. A chapter on annuities will be coming up, but I introduced them here so you could see how the worksheet could help you make some comparisons.

Some people like life annuities so that they will be guaranteed a certain monthly income for the rest of their lives. Fees on annuities can be 8 percent or more *(the exception is fixed annuities, that have lower fees)*.

To reiterate, if you deposited the principal of $724,678 with an insurance company for a lifetime annuity, would they pay you at least $3,969 per month over your lifetime? (If you invested the money and earned 7 percent adjusted for 3 percent inflation, you know you could take out $3,969 per month on average for twenty-three years). However, if the insurance agent's illustration does not make an adjustment for inflation, $5,290 per month would be required to exceed what you could receive for twenty-three years by depositing $724,678 and earning 7 percent on your principal balances. What incentive does the insurance agent offer for you to accept less than that amount? Payments for life? If it is not much less, it might still be a good deal. If it is higher than $5,290 **and** it's for life, jump on it—just don't forget "period certain" and "survivor benefits!"

If you would receive less per month with the life annuity, the difference might be the fees! If you are disciplined and follow a good plan, you could probably get a greater rate of return by investing on your own. But do consider how the annuity might fit into your life's plans and goals. If the insurance company's annuity amount is close to your calculation, absent inflation, and you expect to live beyond twenty-three years, perhaps the annuity would be more profitable. After all, it will be for life. The security of a lifetime annuity can play a role in retirement in certain situations.

Assuming you don't have a defined benefit annuity (fixed pension) coming from work, a *compromise* would be to purchase an annuity that pays 25 or 30 percent of your total monthly retirement income (the three-legged stool). You could create a scenario where one-third of your income would come from social security, one-third from your investments, and one-third from the annuity. That way, you could have some guaranteed income but still have a good part of your investments under your control.

If you have a reasonably sufficient defined benefit pension coming from work (an annuity by definition), you would less likely need an annuity from an insurance company. Unless, of course, the illustrations and terms shown by the insurance company are very attractive. Don't forget, our projections were for a fixed period, to age ninety. So using an alternative to the life annuity only buys you some time as you invest your money well on your own, but you don't want to find yourself close to the predetermined age (90), low on money, and *not have made provisions if it looks like you are going to live well beyond ninety.* You may need to revisit your options as you age.

I wish I could take a firm position like "life annuities are bad because the fees are too high!" But although fees are high, there are other considerations—the comfort and security of receiving income for life. That's why we need to use a spreadsheet with time value of money and interest rate factors or a financial calculator. The spreadsheet above and financial calculator can help you determine how much the insurance company's illustration is *discounting* the stream of payments you could earn for yourself or whether they are paying you a *premium* for the use of your money. If you can take the emotion out of your decision, and it will probably be a better one. Social security income deserves some consideration if you are married.

If you are married and social security is a significant part of family income, be sure to ask the Social Security Administration how much your benefit will be reduced if your spouse passes away and how much your spouse will receive if you pass away first. A surviving spouse who did not work could lose as much as one-third of his or her benefit. If both spouses were workers, the surviving spouse could lose as much as 50 percent of his or her benefit. These factors should be taken into account in life insurance planning. The surviving spouse will need to receive enough insurance to replace the lost social security income for his or her life expectancy.

It is a good idea to leave money invested in the stock market at all times, but you will always need some safe spending money. The following worksheet would be useful in providing for five years of safe spending money. The safe spending money allows you to leave other money invested in the stock market to earn higher rates of return.

MAXIMIZING EARNINGS WHILE PROVIDING SAFETY

Purpose: To Manage Living Expenses During Retirement While Allowing Stock Mutual Funds to Grow

Background: Too many investors sacrifice higher returns to avoid risk. They will own too many bonds and CDs too early and for too long. Since there has seldom been a five year period when stock mutual funds have not rebounded, it would be more profitable to establish a five year cushion of bonds, CDs, and cash and have the balance of investments remain in stock mutual funds.

Procedures: Prior to retirement, create three funds - a combination of cash, CDs, and bonds for five years of living expenses. The balance of investments will remain in stock mutual funds. During retirement, whether you take living expense money from the bonds, CDs, and cash or from the stock mutual funds depends upon how well your stock mutual funds performed the previous 12 months (not necessarily the calendar year). You also will not want to take money out of stock mutual funds when the stock market is currently experiencing a 'correction' or 'crash'.

The order of access will be first cash (saving or checking), then redeem CDs, and lastly bonds. Bonds are a last resort but they are a good source of interest income, better than saving accounts or CDs. Short term or intermediate term corporate bonds are best for this use.

Replenish the cash, bonds, and CDs with money from the stock mutual funds in years when your stock mutual funds have gone up more than say 11%, as a business would refill its petty cash. If your stock mutual funds experienced less than a 11% growth over the most recent year, then live off your cash, CDs, and/or bonds. To be more aggressive, lower the last number to 8 or 9%. To be more conservative, raise the number to 12-13%. (You would only be redeeming stock mutual funds when your rates of return did better than the historical average of the stock market).

Year of Retirement	Your Stock Mutual Funds' Performances	Action Taken	Annual Living Needs	Balances in CDs Bonds & Cash
		Beginning Balances in Bonds, CDs, & Cash	$ 20,000	$ 100,000
1st	8.00%	Live off money from Bonds, CDs, or Cash	$ 20,000	80,000
2nd	-5.00%	Live off money from Bonds, CDs, or Cash	20,000	60,000
3rd	12.00%	Take living expenses from stock mutual funds	20,000	60,000
4th	11.00%	Take living expenses from stock mutual funds	20,000	60,000
5th	14.00%	Take living expenses from stock mutual funds	20,000	60,000
5th	**14.00%**	**Replenish bonds, CDs, & cash from SMF**	40,000	100,000
6th	7.00%	Live off money from Bonds, CDs, or Cash	20,000	80,000
7th	13.00%	Take living expenses from stock mutual funds	20,000	80,000
7th	**13.00%**	**Replenish bonds, CDs, & cash from SMF**	20,000	100,000
8th	-8.00%	Live off money from Bonds, CDs, or Cash	20,000	80,000
9th	12.00%	Take living expenses from stock mutual funds	20,000	80,000
10th	11.00%	Take living expenses from stock mutual funds	20,000	80,000

CHAPTER 12
Education

"The most valuable investment one can make is to cultivate a good mind."

E ducation costs have been rising for decades, but favorable income tax treatment is available if you have low or moderate income. Three good reasons to pursue an education are to improve the mind, enjoy a better quality of life, and create higher income over your lifetime. The good news is U.S. Tax Laws provide tax credits for educational expenses and tax free income on investments made to save for education. The Internal Revenue Service provides a publication on educational expenses (Internal Revenue Service, Pub 970 Educational Expenses). This chapter will focus on two areas:

1. Saving and investing for college and
2. Taking tax credits on your income tax returns.

The two most popular ways to invest and save for college are the Coverdell Education Savings Account (ESA) and Code Section 529 plans. Either or both can be used to invest and save for college. As long as the money is used for school expenses, the withdrawals are free from income taxes.

The Coverdell ESA allows you to invest up to $2,000 per year toward a student's educational expenses. The funds must be used before age thirty but they can be transferred to another child if you like. You get to choose the mutual funds (the underlying accounts for your investment). Fewer mutual fund companies are offering ESAs, so you may have to shop around. The shortcoming of the ESA is that the total contributions to *all* ESA accounts of the beneficiary (the child) in any one year, cannot exceed $2,000.

There are also maximum income requirements on the donors when contributing to an ESA ($110,000 for a single taxpayer, $220,000 for joint returns in 2021). An alternative is to gift the money to a family member with less income (or to the child) and let him or her make the contribution. (But if the child contributes to his or her own ESA that might reduce their potential for federal student aid). A popular alternative with more options is the Code Section 529 plan.

529 plans are more complex and more versatile than ESAs. A 529 plan is an education savings plan operated by a state or educational institution. Like the Coverdell ESAs, earnings on your investments will be tax free if they are used to pay for educational expenses. Qualified educational expenses now include college and certain apprenticeship programs. They also now include elementary and secondary school educational expenses. Allowable expenses include tuition and fees, books, supplies, and equipment. Room and board expenses are allowed if the student attends school at least half-time.

While your contributions are not tax-deductible for *federal* income taxes, most states allow a tax deduction or tax credit on your state's income tax return. Five states so far even allow a deduction for contributions made to another state's 529 plan.

Most 529 plans are flexible and allow you to use them nationwide. That flexibility allows you to have a 529 plan in one state while enabling the student to attend school in another state. To see which plans have the better rates of returns (earnings) and features that meet your goals, visit: https://www.savingforcollege.com/eligible_institutions/.

Important: Whether you choose a 529 plan or an Education Savings Account, you will have to decide which mutual funds to put the investments in. As discussed in the chapter on investing, the longer the time period, the more aggressive you can be. So if the child is very young, you could choose a more aggressive mutual fund than if the child has only a couple of years before he or she will be attending college. Perhaps a balanced fund would be best if there are less than five years before the student will make use of the proceeds from the investment.

The plan manager or broker/dealer will offer you a few mutual funds to choose from. Again, you can handle all these transactions online but I recommend talking with someone from the mutual fund company to be sure you are investing as you intend to.

Qualified Tuition Programs (QTP) also fall under Internal Revenue Code Section 529. A qualified tuition program allows you to either prepay or contribute to an account established for a student's qualified education expenses at an educational institution. QTPs can be established and maintained by states, agencies, or instrumentalities of a state. An eligible educational institution may also set up a QTP.

You may be able to transfer your ESA to a 529 plan. More information is available from www.savingforcollege.com.

Education Tax Credits (Cash Money)
Once you or your loved ones are attending college or other institutions of higher learning, you will likely be able to take advantage of tax credits on your federal income tax returns. You may want to first determine whether it is better for the student or parents to take the credits by preparing drafts of both returns (if necessary). You may want to determine which way benefits the family more. If the student is in the zero or 10-percent tax bracket, and the parents are in the 25-percent or higher bracket, the parent will usually get a greater tax saving than the student. For the parents to take the credit, they must provide more than one-half of the student's support *and* carry the student as a dependent (it's okay if the student is away at college).

Sometimes young people might be eager to file their first income tax return and that might create a conflict. There is a box to check on the first page of the *student's* tax return, where he or she indicates they *"may be claimed as a dependent on someone else's return."* If the student fails to check that box (in effect claiming an exemption for himself) it will be necessary for him to file an amended return (1040X) so that the parent can validly claim the student as a dependent (and take the credit). Otherwise, the parent will get a letter from the IRS, and explanations, amended returns, and headaches are bound to follow.

To avoid the above, I encourage parents to communicate with their young students early in January before they even get their Form W-2s, before they have an opportunity to file their tax returns. You have to work out whether the child will be claimed as a dependent and who will benefit more from claiming the education credits. If the parent takes the credit, why not give the student a portion of the tax savings as a reward for cooperation? (Cash has a way of gaining cooperation).

In consideration of the above, the credit begins to phase out when your modified adjusted gross income is between 80,000 and $90,000 for a single person and between 160,000 and $180,000 if you are married filing jointly (above $180,000 the credit would be zero). In such cases perhaps the child whose income is lower could benefit from taking the credits.

The **American Opportunity Tax Credit** is available for the first four years of college. For the year 2021, this can mean up to $2,500 of credit against your taxes (for each eligible student).

The amount of the credit is 100 percent of the first $2,000 of qualified education expenses and 25 percent of the next $2,000 paid per student. If the credit brings your tax liability down to *zero*, you can still get 40 percent of any remaining amount refunded to you (up to $1,000).

After you (or the student) have claimed the American Opportunity Tax Credit for four years, you now have available the **Lifetime Learning Credit (LLC)**. There is no limit on the number of years you can claim the LLC. It is worth up to $2,000 per tax year.

Until the year 2019, if your Adjusted Gross Income was too high to allow you to take the credits, you were able to take a *deduction* for your educational expenses on page one of the 1040, but that deduction went away for tax years 2020 and beyond. Maybe Congress will bring that back one day?

Stay tuned.

When the student has income, he or she may be able to deduct up to $2,500 of interest expense paid on student loans.

An area more complicated than paying for college is annuities.

CHAPTER 13

Annuities

Dependable Income for a Price

Annuities can be useful in retirement planning under certain conditions, but first, some definitions may be helpful:

1. The **Contract Owner** is the person who purchases the contract (he may or may not be the annuitant).
2. The **Annuitant** is the person expected to receive the payouts from the annuity.
3. The **Beneficiary** is someone who will receive any residual benefits if the Annuitant dies prematurely.
4. **Accumulation Phase** is the period when the contract owner funds (or pays into) the annuity contract.
5. **Payout period** is when the annuitant receives payments. The payment can be immediate (all paid next month or year), paid over a period of time, paid for life, or for a fixed amount.

The reasons for buying an annuity include:

+ To provide a lifetime of guaranteed income
+ To possibly increase your income in retirement
+ To save for the long term
+ To invest in a program that defers taxes on investment earnings

- To supplement your social security or other retirement plans; and
- If you are nearing fifty or older, it may be a cost-effective means of getting long-term care insurance coverage.

Like many financial planning illustrations, most prevailing annuity models assume the client has adequate money to make contributions in either a lump sum or periodic payments and the resulting payouts will be sufficient to meet the client's future income needs. But what if the client has minimal resources, and his or her contributions during the accumulation phase of the contract will not result in a high enough stream of payouts to meet the client's future living needs? What if the expenses of the (lifetime) annuity pull down the future annuity payments to an unacceptable level? In such a case, investing in no-load mutual funds on your own may be a desirable option. But depending upon your lifestyle, available resources, and risk tolerance, the guarantee of a lifetime stream of income could make the annuity an attractive choice. (Also, see the worksheet and discussion at the end of the chapter on Retirement).

There are different types of annuities:

1. **Fixed Annuities** pay out an agreed amount over a period of time or lifetime. The interest payments will be higher than savings accounts or CDs but not as high as the potential on stock market returns. The rates of returns may not be high enough to cover inflation. They are less expensive than other annuities and are okay for retired persons who want to receive a fixed payment for a fixed period of time, say five or ten years. Single-premium fixed deferred annuities (one payment from you) usually pay out a higher interest rate. The risk of payments is with the insurance company.

2. **Variable Annuities** allow the owner to select the mutual funds that "underlie" the investment. These *sub accounts* may contain stocks and bonds. Only the portion of your premiums paid to the "fixed" account are guaranteed to be paid by the insurance company. The investment is similar to a savings account that has an

opportunity to realize stock market and bond market earnings on the portion of the premiums invested in the *non-fixed* accounts, the sub accounts. Note that these sub accounts are subject to stock or bond market ups and downs with no guarantees of return of principal (the investment component of your premium).

A variable annuity may be a good option for someone who wants to *defer* income taxes on earnings and has maxed out his or her IRA or 401K contributions. The variable annuity may be good for a younger person (who can afford it) who likes the potential growth of the stock market and doesn't mind the risk. Just be sure you can leave the money in until age 59 & 1/2.

3. **Equity-Index Annuities** are also called fixed index annuities. They have the feature of partial participation in a stock market index(-like the Fortune 500 Index) . They provide safety and guarantee of principal and earnings. Participation rates in an index will vary; for instance, a contract may allow the annuity to participate at 85 percent of the gain of the Fortune 500 Index. There may be a cap rate—a maximum percentage increase allowed in a year. How the increases are calculated and when earnings are credited to your account will vary. Some may credit earnings annually; others may not for *six or seven* years! Many index annuities will have an early surrender charge. But you should not be charged an investment advisory fee since index funds are not managed.

4. **Split Annuities** combine one or more annuities. One of the annuities is designed to provide monthly income over a set period of time. The second annuity is designed to grow back to the original invested amount using fixed interest payments from the insurance company.

Annuity premiums (or your contributions) in the accumulation stage can be a single premium (lump sum), or they can be periodic. If periodic, they can be flexible or level (fixed) premiums.

Annuity payments (or your withdrawals) can be immediate or deferred over time. With an immediate annuity, payments begin one month or one year after the accumulation period ends. The payments can be paid to one annuitant, straight joint life with survivor benefits, or joint life *without* survivor benefits. With the joint life *without survivor benefits*, payments stop when the first spouse dies. In such a joint life without survivor benefits plan, the surviving spouse would be expected to live off life insurance proceeds from the first spouse to pass. There can also be a period-certain with refund option, where a beneficiary receives full payment of the premiums paid if the annuitant (spouse) dies before a certain period ends (i.e., inside of ten years).

Annuities have several costs. There are sales charges, mortality expense fees (related to the potential life expectancy of the annuitant), and management fees. Some states even have a 2-percent tax for regulating annuities. If these fees are not spelled out in the illustrations presented by the insurance agent, it is hard to measure their impact on the payout. The lifetime annuity (where the insurance company agrees to pay throughout the annuitant's lifetime) will have several charges since this is where the insurance company assumes the most risk. Variable annuities will have annual administrative charges for maintenance and mortality expense, plus investment advisory fees on the sub accounts. They also carry a surrender charge designed to discourage the contract owner from discontinuing the contract. Some companies may allow 10 percent of the contract be withdrawn after one year for emergencies. The surrender charge provision may last on a declining scale for up to ten years.

Some companies offer cost-of-living riders that help with inflation. Other riders include a guaranteed minimum death benefit and a guaranteed minimum withdrawal benefit. One rider that should receive consideration is the long-term care option. With the LTC option, the insurance company would use the accumulated value of the annuity to pay nursing home costs. If there is also the flexibility of paying for in-home care, this could be an attractive feature. Traditional long-term care policies have become very expensive, and the need for long-term care is a serious possibility for most of us.

Remember, there is also a 10-percent tax penalty for withdrawing cash from the annuity before age 59 & 1/2. Most contracts provide a "Free Look Period" that gives you thirty days to cancel the annuity contract (for any reason).

Let's look at some considerations of life annuities. You may want one if:

1. You don't think you can be a good investor on your own
2. You don't think you can exercise discipline in your spending
3. The long-term care rider seems a bargain compared to other LTC options
4. You are conservative and don't want to take much risk; and
5. The expected payouts shown in the insurance agent's illustrations seem adequate to meet your future income needs (even with future inflation).

However! If most of the above doesn't line up, especially if the expected payouts provide less income than you will need, perhaps investing in no-load stock mutual funds on your own is the way to go. Try to project (using a financial calculator) how much more per month you could pay yourself by earning a reasonable 7 percent on your investment. That will mean exercising some discipline over your investing and spending and taking on risks yourself, but I think this option is better than buying an inadequate annuity you will not be happy with. Investment concepts are covered in detail in the chapter on investing.

In the retirement chapter, you will see how investing on your own can grow over time using an 11-percent rate of return (calculating your nest egg). After the nest egg is calculated, you can estimate how much you can withdraw monthly over what you believe will be a reasonable life expectancy. This second calculation is similar to calculating a mortgage payment by entering the nest egg (or principal), interest rate (or earnings rate of 7 percent), and number of years or months involved—the duration.

By doing your own calculations with a spreadsheet or financial calculator, you can compare those projected monthly payouts on your investments to the annuity payouts the insurance agent shows in his or her illustrations.

If you already have an annuity and an insurance agent proposes to exchange the annuity for another, he or she is required to use a checklist to see if the new annuity's features are superior to the old one.

Finally, when purchasing an annuity, be sure the prospective insurance company has at least a B++/B+ rating with A.M. Best or Moody's. If they are unrated, determine why? You don't want to give your money to a company that may not be around to live up to its obligations.

Remember, using an alternative to the life annuity only buys you some time as you invest your money on your own, but you don't want to find yourself close to a predetermined age (say age ninety), low on money, and *not have made provisions if it looks like you are going to live well beyond that age.* So you may need to revisit your options as time passes and you get more experience with your finances. Keep making good decisions with the help of trusted friends and loved ones. Health savings accounts can be another effective way of saving and reducing taxes during your working years.

CHAPTER 14
Health Savings Accounts

Health Savings Accounts (HSAs) are covered because they could save you some income taxes and get stock market rates of returns on the amounts saved (or invested). The HSA is also a good place to save for medical, dental, vision, and pharmaceutical expenses. You should have the ability to invest your contributions into stock mutual funds—mutual funds with the history of excellent growth.

HSAs are *not* a substitute for a health insurance plan, even though some politicians suggest they are a way of financing health care costs. They probably don't believe their own words. For one thing, most people living on low or moderate incomes do not have thousands of dollars to contribute to a health savings account. Even if they did, that wouldn't cover more than 10 percent of their actual health care costs! Have these politicians even seen the charges for one night in a hospital? Ten years ago, my overnight bill was $120,000, and all the tests came back negative—probably just something I ate! The motive of these politicians is simply to float the idea that Americans can have health care with little or no government subsidies. But let's look at the contributions allowed to an HSA and some of the things you can use it for.

For the tax year 2022, the maximum a single person could contribute to an HSA is $3,650. The maximum a couple could contribute is $7,300. If you are over fifty-five, you could contribute an additional $1,000, with the so-called "catch-up" provision. Many, if not most, people don't even contribute these amounts to an HSA. Perhaps their budgets are too small or

HSAs were not readily available to them. But an HSA can result in some tax-savings, and the investment can grow and be profitable.

HSAs are treated as pre-tax items for income tax purposes—the contributions are subtracted from your wages and not included in your taxable income. HSAs can be used by self-employed persons too (you would have to set one up yourself with a no-load mutual fund company). As long as your withdrawals are made for medically related expenses (that's medical providers, *pharmacies*, or other medical or dental expenses), the withdrawals will not be taxable to you.

HSA withdrawals can be used to pay Part B Medicare premiums and long-term care insurance premiums. In summary, you can benefit from lowering your taxable wages with the contribution and pay no tax on the appreciation in the investment value that resulted from your contribution! If you choose appropriate investments, your HSA should grow very well. See IRS Publication 969 for more information on Health Savings Accounts. HSAs may not make you wealthy, but they can be a very profitable use of money for working people. Every little bit helps.

Of much bigger impact on our health and finances is managing health care in our senior years. I'm thinking about the choice between Medicare Advantage and Medigap (*Medicare Supplement*) plans.

CHAPTER 15
Medicare, Medicare Advantage, & Medigap Plans

W e have three main options for medical care insurance when we turn sixty-five, but only Medicare Advantage and Medigap (Medicare Supplement) are viable options unless we qualify for Medicaid. To qualify for Medicaid, your income has to be extremely low, and the Medicaid programs in some states may be lacking. If you have to rely on Medicaid, your health is at risk if you live in a state that does not participate in Medicaid expansion. Twelve governors did not participate in Medicaid expansion as of August 2022: Wyoming, Texas, South Dakota, Wisconsin, Mississippi, Tennessee, Alabama, Georgia, North Carolina, South Carolina, Kansas, and Florida. Traditional *Medicare* is a basic coverage available when you turn age sixty-five. Veterans may also have the option for treatment at a VA Hospital but I chose not to address Veteran's health care because it is so complicated and not everyone qualifies.

There is usually no premium for Medicare **Part A**. It covers hospitals, skilled nursing, hospice, and most home health care costs (one hundred days maximum). The coverage is automatic for seniors at age sixty-five if they qualify. The coverage is also available if you become disabled before age sixty-five. To qualify for Medicare, you must have paid into Medicare for at least ten years (consistent with the qualifications for Social Security benefits).

Medicare **Part B** insurance covers doctors, outpatient services, and other medically necessary expenses. Part B is voluntary, and premium payments are usually deducted from your social security check. **If you fail to sign up for Part B when you first become eligible for it, your premiums will increase by 10 percent for each twelve months that you delay.** One signs up for Part B at a local Social Security Office. Medicare **Part D**, was introduced in 2006 and covers prescription drugs.

Because Medicare does not cover all medical costs, additional plans came along to fill the gap. One group includes the **Medicare Advantage** plans (Part C Plans). These plans are provided by private insurers and cover hospitals and doctors. They create a ton of TV advertisements and mailers especially during "open season" (mid-October to early December).

To participate, you must be enrolled in Medicare Part A and Part B and continue to pay your Part B premiums. Each Medicare Advantage plan has its own network of doctors, hospitals, home health agencies, and skilled nursing facilities. Some plans include prescription drugs (although there could be a separate premium payment for drug coverage). Services are bundled (all-in-one). Medicare Advantage plans usually include free gym membership and the Silver Sneakers program.

Medicare *Advantage* plans may also provide health services through HMOs or PPOs (Managed Plans and Preferred Providers). With PPO plans, you may not need to select a primary care doctor or need referrals to see a specialist, but you could still have higher costs for doctors not in the plan's network.

There are *risk* plans and *cost* plans. With risk plans, you get all your coverage through the plan or referrals. You are "locked in." Any treatment you receive outside of the plan will *not* be paid or only partially paid. With a *cost* plan, you are not locked in. You can go outside of the plan, and at least Medicare will pay approved charges, but you will be responsible for any co-pays or deductibles. Cost plans might be better if you travel a lot.

The prescription drug benefit is also available through a Medicare Advantage plan. Premiums (if applicable) will vary depending upon your location and plan. Covered persons pay a percentage of the drug costs, and Medicare pays the balance. Your cost for prescription drugs would not usually exceed 25 percent of the drug costs.

Prescription drug coverage may also be obtained through Prescription Drug Plans (PDPs). PDPs may be available through employers and employer retirement plans.

Premiums are generally low for Medicare Advantage plans, ranging from zero to fifty dollars per month. But you *must* see doctors in your service area to avoid out-of-network fees. You will need referrals for specialty doctors.

Although premiums are low, you will have co-pays, co-insurance, and deductibles to deal with, and while your out-of-pocket costs are capped at about $6,700 annually, prescription drug costs do not count toward that cap. That makes it hard to budget for medical expenses with Medicare Advantage plans. Medicare Advantage plans compete with Medicare *Supplement* Plans (Medigap).

Medigap plans, also called **Medicare Supplement Plans, are** another alternative to the original Medicare, senior medical coverage. You have six months to sign up for a Medigap policy from the time you sign up for Medicare Part B. Medigap coverage is *comprehensive*. Medigap policies have standardized language regarding the benefits they cover. As the chart below shows, these coverages range from A through N with "F" having more benefits than the other options. But "F" policies are no longer being sold (though existing "F" policies are still honored). Popular benefits covered by most plans include your Part A and Part B deductibles, co-insurance, preventive care, and so on. Comparison shop and pay attention to the benefits most important to you. Foreign travel coverage might be helpful if you travel a lot. The plans will include a thirty-day "free look"—in case you want to cancel.

The premiums on a Medicare Supplement plan will be higher than a Medicare Advantage program. They currently range from $120 to $150 per month. You may also have a separate premium for prescription drug coverage, about $30 per month. But you will have no co-pays, co-insurance, or out-of-pocket deductibles with most plans. Also, you are not limited in the doctors you can see. **So which plans are better? Medicare Advantage or Medigap (*the so called Medicare Supplement plans*)?**

I come down on the side of the Medicare Supplement plans (Medigap). While you will have lower monthly premiums with Medicare Advantage plans, after co-pays, co-insurance, and out-of-pocket deductibles of up to $8,100 annually for a family, you can easily exceed the $150 per month premium you might pay for a Medicare Supplement plan ($120 + $30 drug coverage). Another factor of major concern with Medicare Advantage plans is being responsible for out-of-network costs you might run into while traveling. From a health maintenance standpoint, if we are too concerned with avoiding co-pays and specialty charges, we might not seek the help that we need. I believe the benefit of seeing any doctor I might need to see is very important.

Consider your budget, lifestyle, and health needs in making this decision. You might also go to Medicare.gov and explore the many plans available in your area and their benefits. This can be an overwhelming exercise, so list what's most important to *you* before starting your research. In considering Medicare Advantage plans, you will want to know whether your favorite doctors are included in the network.

A couple of cautionary notes: If you leave a Medicare Supplement plan and go into a managed care or Medicare Advantage plan and want to return to a Medicare Supplement plan, you could experience difficulties if you have developed health issues. They could deny you coverage or charge a higher premium because you now have a pre-existing condition. So it might not be a good idea to switch back and forth if you are at risk for a medical diagnosis.

If you are retired military and are entitled to Tricare for Life, that is in fact your Medicare Supplement plan. But you could lose that benefit if you do not sign up for Medicare Part B when you turn age 65. Even if you are still working and have a health care plan at work that you prefer to use, you must sign up for Medicare Part B and pay the premiums to avoid losing your Tricare for Life entitlement.

Some popular Medigap (Supplement) plans include AARP, Blue Cross, Humana, and more.

| Medigap Plans A-N | | | | | | | | | | |
Medicare Supplements	A	B	C	D	F	G	K	L	M	N
Basic Benefits	X	X	X	X	X	X	50%	75%	X	X
Part B, Co-insurance	X	X	X	X	X	X	50%	75%	X	Copay
Skilled Nursing			X	X	X	X	50%	75%	X	X
Part A, Deductible		X	X	X	X	X	50%	75%	50%	X
Part B, Deductible			X		X					
Part B Excess					100%	100%				
Foreign Travel			X	X	X	X			X	X
Preventive Care	X	X	X	X	X	X	X	X	X	X

Note that Plans C and F are no longer sold after December 31, 2019. Policies purchased before that date may be honored and renewed.

Massachusetts, Minnesota, and Wisconsin have waivers and are permitted by statute to have different standardized plans.

Medicare is closely related to social security. Next, we look at when is the best time to start drawing it.

CHAPTER 16

When to Draw Social Security

S ocial security can be complicated, so let's begin with some facts and
simple recommendations.

1. If you don't need social security at age sixty-two, wait until at least
    your full retirement age or even longer to draw it (full retirement
    age is sixty-seven in most cases).
2. Age eighty seems to be the statistical break-even point. That is, if
    you live past eighty, you will receive more benefits over your life-
    time by waiting until your full retirement age. If you take your
    benefit at sixty-two it will be about 25 percent less than you would
    receive per month at your full retirement age. That's 25 percent less
    for the rest of your life.
3. If you are experiencing a serious illness that may shorten your life
    span, perhaps you should take it sooner rather than later.

We could end this chapter right here. The advice above will not change.
But let's discuss what's necessary to qualify, the financial risks of taking
social security before full retirement age, and the 7–8 percent per year
increase in your benefit by waiting longer to draw social security.

To be fully qualified to draw social security, you will need to accumulate forty quarters (credits) of minimum earnings (the equivalent of
ten working years). In the year 2022, one credit is earned for every $1,510

of wages earned. So the earnings required to get four credits in 2022 was $6,040.

Age sixty-two is considered early retirement. If you take social security at age sixty-two and are still working, earnings from wages above a certain amount ($19,560 in 2022) can require you to pay back **50 percent** of the social security benefits you received above that earnings threshold. If you are still working, this is a disincentive to taking social security early. Additionally, if you are single and earn more than $25,000, some of your social security may be taxable ($32,000 if married filing jointly). What a major mess if you didn't need the money in the first place! Plus, you are stuck with that monthly payment for life because cost-of-living increases to social security since the 1980s have been small (with the exception of 2021).

The full retirement age for people born after 1960 is sixty-seven. It's a little less than age sixty-seven if you were born before 1960 (please consult the first link below to connect to a chart showing your exact full retirement age if you were born before 1960). If you take social security at sixty-two, you will receive a *permanent* reduction of 25 to 30 percent in your monthly benefit compared to what you would receive at full retirement age. This is a big reason not to take social security early.

For each year you wait to collect *after* reaching your full retirement age, your benefit continues to increase by 8 percent per year until age 70. No other investment guarantees an 8 percent annual increase in its rate of return! So if you are in a position to wait until age seventy, your benefit will be approximately 24 percent higher than you would get at your full retirement age (assuming it was age sixty-seven). You can still take it at sixty-eight or sixty-nine and enjoy the 8-percent per year increase over what you would have received at age sixty-seven.

If you are still working *or* have pension distributions that exceed your budgetary needs, that may be another reason to wait until later. Then you can avoid the social security payments placing you into a higher tax bracket and paying taxes on your social security benefits. Why take the money out, pay taxes on it, and then try to figure out where to invest it when all you had to do was leave it alone and let it grow by 8 percent per year? Waiting in this scenario assumes you don't need the money, your health is good, and you expect to live beyond age eighty. If you are healthy and plan to work beyond age 70, you may want to wait closer to age 70 to draw it. That's because your earnings are always subject to social security tax withholdings and the additional earnings may increase your benefit amount. Just know that your social security benefit doesn't increase after you reach age 70 even though social security and Medicare withholding are still required. I think that is taxation without representation! Help us out AARP.

The Social Security Administration (SSA) used to mail us annual benefit estimates, showing how much we would receive at different ages (assuming our future wages stayed the same). Now we have to sign up with SSA.gov and log in to see those statements and estimates. It is worth doing.

It is clear that the longer you wait to collect social security, the higher your benefit will be. I know some people say, "I'm going to take social security as soon as I can because there is no guarantee it will be there!" Well, what if they are wrong and it *is* there? How much have they hurt *themselves* financially? This is a financial debate, not a political one. My recommendation is simple. If you need the money early to avoid poverty, take it. If you don't believe you have a life expectancy beyond age eighty, take it. Otherwise, postpone it as long as you can (but not past age 70). Senior citizens are a strong voting bloc. Congress will figure out what to do to strengthen the Social Security trust fund.

A worker's survivors may also receive benefits. If a worker's surviving spouse cares for a child under age 16, he or she could receive 50 percent of the worker's benefit. The benefit will also be available if the child becomes disabled before reaching age twenty-two. The children of a deceased worker may be eligible if they are unmarried and under age eighteen (or nineteen— if they are still in high school). The child's benefit will also be 50 percent of the worker's benefit payments.

Divorced spouses may receive a benefit based on their ex-spouse's entitlement as long as they were married at least 10 years and have not remarried. They also have to be at least sixty-two years of age.

This was only a brief coverage of social security. I tried to cover what most people need to know about drawing social security. If your situation is more complicated, consider speaking with a social security specialist. For instance, if your spouse was deceased after age sixty-two and you want to draw his or her benefit until you are age seventy, or if one spouse is a great deal older than the other, or one spouse has reached retirement age and the other has not. In these situations, you may want to speak with counselors who specialize in Social Security benefits or arrange an appointment with your local Social Security Office to see which options are best for you.

Links below can help you determine your projected benefits.

https://www.ssa.gov/policy/docs/ssb/v74n4/v74n4p21.html
(full retirement age chart)

https://www.ssa.gov/benefits/retirement/estimator.html

https://www.consumerfinance.gov/consumer-tools/retirement/before-you-claim/

Social Security Calculator: Estimate Your Benefits (aarp.org)

Have you ever wondered how many of today's negative attitudes towards taxes and government were shaped?

CHAPTER 17
Reverse Robin Hood and the Taxman

"Don't Tax You, Don't Tax Me, Tax the Man behind the Tree!"

President Reagan was popular for his charismatic and casual speaking style. He took a hard stance against communism and his relationship with Mikhail Gorbachev helped bring about major turning points in the Cold War. His tax cuts decreased unemployment and inflation, but many anti-government attitudes of today might also be traced to the Reagan Administration. President Reagan, speaking from his podium, said, "The nine most terrifying words in the English language are—I'm from the government and I'm here to help" (10). He added, "Government can't solve the problem, government *is* the problem". As Fareed Zakaria of CNN said in his television program discussing America's crumbling infrastructure, "Reagan's defunding, dismantling, and demeaning of government has taken its toll." (11)

It was during the Reagan Administration that the idea of cutting taxes on high-income earners to achieve economic growth became acceptable economic policy with the Republican Party. Supply-side, trickle-down economics then became the mantra of the Republican Party. The idea was that tax reductions on high income earners would provide businesses with more money, they would use that money to manufacture more goods, and people would buy those goods, resulting in economic growth and greater tax revenues. But 35 years of experience is proof that "Reaganomics' did not do much of what its proponents claimed it would.

President Reagan's tax cuts gave birth to the government deficit spending policies and debt that we are struggling with today. Following Reagan into office, the first President Bush acted responsibly by raising taxes to deal with the budget deficit. Then his fellow republicans disparaged him so badly that he was unable to generate enough support to get reelected. He lost the election to Bill Clinton. President Clinton also raised taxes and yet enjoyed record job growth, higher wages, higher gross domestic product, a strong stock market, and lower unemployment!

As I look back, I heard less grumbling about income taxes in the 1960s and 1970s than I hear today. That was true for people from most income brackets. While people did complain about taxes, it was in jest, not in anger and frustration as today. It was a way of bonding, making small talk, identifying with the working class. The small amounts withheld from our paychecks came back to us when we filed our tax returns anyway.

After President Reagan lowered the top tax rate from 70 percent to only 28 percent in the 1980s, financial professionals could have turned their attention to the needs of those with lower incomes, those whose wealth didn't increase with the tax cuts, but they didn't. They continued to focus instead on methods to help higher-income individuals pay even less income taxes.

So a lot of knowledge, training, and experience has been used to help those less in need of financial help. As a result, the reputations of financial professionals have suffered. Financial professionals seldom address *state* income taxes, sales taxes, property taxes, and utility rates that have all skyrocketed since the 1980s. Understand that those state and local tax increases correlate with the federal income tax cuts of the 1980s.

The middle class today is frustrated with the many tax increases that have fallen on our backs over the past forty years. A significant increase in taxes on the middle class has been the loss of federal income tax deductions. In implementing President Reagan's tax cuts, Congress also performed *tax simplification*. They gave the middle class a higher standard deduction but took away many helpful deductions the middle class enjoyed (President

Trump did the same thing in 2017, but his higher standard deductions will expire in 2025).

Though President Reagan's higher standard deductions seemed a generous compromise to simplify the tax code at the time, Congress's annual increase in the standard deductions has not kept up with inflation. President Reagan (and Congress) took some deductions away from those with higher incomes too, but that was largely symbolic since their tax rates were cut more than half. Meanwhile, those in the middle class were less able to lose the specific deductions taken away from them. For instance, even though medical costs have skyrocketed since the 1980s, Congress has made it nearly impossible for *anyone* to deduct medical expenses.

The Tax Reform Acts of the 1980s took away the interest expense deduction, except for mortgage interest. People with low and moderate income use a lot of credit! I'm not advocating more use of credit; I'm only reporting that the tax deduction was of great benefit to those with low and moderate income whether they were homeowners or not.

Congress has practically disallowed employee business expenses. When employee business expenses were fully deductible, we got tax help for performing our jobs or paying for school that improved our worth to employers. We were able to deduct the costs of tools and training. And teachers could deduct the hundreds of dollars they spent helping kids in their classrooms (thousands in today's dollars).

In 2019, the Employee Business Expense deduction was taken away from most people, though most people haven't been able to use it since the 1980s anyway after the expense became an itemized deduction, with 10 percent of our adjusted gross income subtracted from it. Then in 2020, Congress disallowed it until 2026. Even then, because of its treatment as an itemized deduction, most people won't be able to deduct those expenses anyway.

Moving expenses have now been disallowed too—except for the military—who already get reimbursed for moving expenses! That sounds military friendly but is simply brilliant politics! While military members are busy running around the world serving our country, they probably won't notice that sleight of hand. For a long time, when your spouse passed away, you were able to file as Head of Household for two additional years (to lower your taxable income). That was the law for four decades. Congress took that benefit away in the 1990s. So over the past 40 years folks living with middle and low income have lost federal tax deductions while simultaneously experiencing increases in state and local taxes!

In 1981, the State of Connecticut had the highest sales tax rate in the country (7.5 percent combined city and state). Connecticut's sales tax rate was high, but it was tolerated because Connecticut did not have a state income tax, except on capital gains and dividends. (*I actually worked in that department*). Fast forward to 2022 and *most* states now have sales tax rates <u>higher</u> than 7.5 percent. Connecticut today has a 6.35 percent sales tax rate, but it also now has a state income tax rate averaging 5.7 percent!

Not only have states raised income and sales tax rates but "fees" have been added to our utility bills that were not there before the 1980s! States, cities, counties, and utilities had to make up the revenue lost after the federal government cut funding to them in the mid-1980s. With all the revenue the federal government lost with the tax cuts, Congress cut their funding. I don't think I have even heard the term *revenue sharing* in the last thirty years!

Many politicians will run for public office on a platform of cutting taxes. "I will fight to cut (*income*) taxes" they retort. But while income tax rates have come down significantly for the top 1 percent since the 1980s, Social Security withholding, state income taxes, and every other tax or fee you can think of has increased significantly. And folks with low and moderate income can least afford to pay them!

We sometimes hear that the wealthy get favorable tax treatment and wonder why there are fewer tax strategies for low and middle income workers. And I think to myself, who are people voting for? And do we know who is really pulling the strings of the politicians we voted for? Democratic Administrations do not target the middle class or low income workers with their tax increases. Conversely, Republican Administrations seldom target low and moderate income earners with their tax cuts! Some 86% of President Trump's tax cuts went to the top 1 percent!

The anti-government sentiment and divisiveness in the U. S. exploded after the elimination of the Fairness Doctrine in broadcasting. Passed in 1949, this doctrine required media outlets to present opinions from both sides in cases where media outlets were *not* simply reporting straight, *factual* news. The absence of this doctrine has allowed anti-government ideology to be spread on the radio, TV, and internet without the balance of dissenting voices. The Federal Communication Commission abolished the Fairness Doctrine during the Reagan Administration. Today, people can hear right-wing propaganda twenty-four hours a day by a TV network that calls itself News. As evidenced by the speeches leading up to the insurrection at the US Capitol on January 6, 2021, words have power and can lead to negative consequences.

While Republican candidates for office gain notoriety through complaining about immigrants crossing our southern border, the immigrant invited to fly in and buy a major newspaper company poses a much greater threat to democracy. After reneging on his promise to keep the newspaper liberal, the individual in question supported a Republican candidate for President; saw his application for American citizenship fast-tracked; received a waiver to US laws prohibiting ownership of both a newspaper and a television station; then bought a major television network that dominates TV ratings.

You would think prohibiting ownership of both a newspaper and a television network would be a conservative idea. That separation makes it difficult to have a monopoly on news coverage and leaves room for diversity of thought and ideas. Likewise, conserving the planet, its natural resources, and living within one's means would be conservative ideas. But the leadership of the Republican Party is not concerned with conserving anything of meaning to the average American. Their goal in the last 40 years and today has been about acquiring power. And if cutting taxes that mostly benefit their doners helps keep them in power, taxes will be cut in their favor in spite of all other needs, consequences, and considerations.

The American economy has not been served well by cutting taxes on the top 1 percent. Cutting taxes might spur economic growth to a certain extent and for a short period of time. The evidence over the past thirty-five years proves that our economy suffers from a state of under-taxation (look at the debt and annual deficits). Blame it on spending if you like, but the social security safety net and Medicare health care coverage are good uses of money. And if you cut education or military spending you will upset some other Americans!

The American economy is a dynamic, complex organism that grows and contracts; speeds up and slows down. And politicians use those economic cycles as a means to criticize their opponents.

In plain words, the Federal Reserve (The Fed) handles economic policy. They attempt to keep unemployment and inflation low. By raising the interest rates, they help curb inflation. By lowering interest rates, the economy is allowed to grow, unemployment is reduced, and recessions are avoided. One reason the Fed kept interest rates so low until 2022 was it didn't want to interfere with economic growth. But the combination of high government and private spending and supply chain issues led to historic jumps in inflation. So in 2021 and 2022 the Fed raised interest rates to help curb inflation.

The President and Congress also impact the economy by increasing or decreasing the supply of money, raising or lowering taxes, or increasing or decreasing spending. With so many cooks in the kitchen it is difficult to predict cycles of economic growth, recessions, unemployment, and inflation. Plus the effect of a policy change may not even be seen for several months. None of the above has anything to do with communism or socialism!

Economic cycles are similar to cooking on an electric stove: the heat rises and falls; just when you think you need to turn up the heat, the pot boils over! Many events cause the economic cycle's ups and downs, periods of growth and recession. Yet people who don't understand economics (or electricity) use loud megaphones to scare us about socialism, communism, and any other *ism* in an effort to protect concentrated wealth and power.

The top 1 percent has not only seen their income taxes reduced significantly, but *estate* taxes have come down sharply too. A lot of brain power has been used to help a couple of thousand people minimize their federal estate taxes, even though that tax only applies to couples leaving behind more than 24 million dollars.

Maybe our perspectives on taxes were shaped by the tale of Robin Hood, where he stole from the tax-collecting sheriff and gave to the poor. Though the tale has sentimental value, there was no middle class and no people voting for slick-talking politicians who secretly represented the Sheriff. There was no Congress in the Robin Hood story. In our real-life story, there is no Robin Hood giving to the poor! There is only Congress (the Sheriff) collecting taxes from the middle class to protect the abundance of the few. Through *our* choices for Congress and President, we have voted to reduce the king's taxes, while raising our own.

Having your own business can provide opportunities to reach financial independence.

CHAPTER 18

How to Organize a Business:

Business—The Ticket for Admission to Financial Independence

R unning a successful business can be a significant undertaking. Before you spend a lot of money on a business venture, it is best to write a business plan. It can be just a brief five to ten page document that outlines your business goals and visions. It would include the resumes and capabilities of key personnel, marketing and business strategies, projected cash flows, competition, income tax structure, and so on. Your initial business plan does not have to be so elaborate it will persuade others to invest in your company, but it does need to include enough thought and detail so that when *you* look at it, *you* still believe the business has the potential to succeed.

A few days spent in creating a business plan will prepare you for the first big challenges to come your way. Also, if the business plan shows that the market environment or projected earnings and cash flows are not positive, you have a chance to reconsider before investing more time and money into the venture. If your plan will involve significant start-up costs and you anticipate the need for investors, potential partners will usually expect you to put up at least 25 percent of the start-up cash.

You can find templates for business plans on the web or you can use a Word template. For a more detailed or professional plan, you could enlist the help of SCORE (Service Corps of Retired Executives). You might be able to get the help from a business or marketing student from a local university or community college. It could take a couple of months before the help is available, so put your requests in early. Many colleges and universities affiliate with small business development centers sponsored by the city or not-for-profit organizations. The Small Business Administration can also be helpful. Many states and cities support small business development and may potentially be a source for contracts depending upon your line of business.

If you are a veteran, the VA has resources to help veteran business owners. And veterans like to do business with other veterans!

Once we have begun to form an image of a successful business, let's get it off on the right foot. If you have a business or intend to begin one, the most important thing you need to do is **separate your business accounts and transactions from your personal accounts and transactions!** If you use credit cards, get a separate credit card for your business activities. Even if the business's name is not on the separate credit card, or separate checking accounts, at least the transactions would be separated from your personal expenses.

Even the best accountants will have difficulty extracting your business transactions from your personal transactions and that work is not of any value to the business. Let your advisors help you with more important things. Not only are separate accounts a requirement of the IRS, but if you comingle business with personal transactions, you run the risk of overpaying or underpaying taxes. Significant mistakes in *either* direction could cause business failure and personal hardship.

Before or as soon as your business activities begin expanding, invest in a good accounting system. If you decide you want to use QuickBooks or other low-cost accounting software to do the accounting yourself, hire a reputable accountant or QuickBooks professional to set up your accounting system. They will help you set up your database of clients, vendors, employees, the chart of accounts, ledgers, and codes for the products and services you offer. If you expect to have a significant number of transactions per year (in the thousands), consider having a full-time person with accounting skills on board.

As soon as your business can sustain one, hire an accountant or book-keeper (whether or not you do the accounting in-house). If you don't think you need a full-time person, you might be able to contract out the accounting for your business (remember, if you want to do your own books, it's easier for everyone if the books are set up right to begin with).

Unfortunately some accounting software vendors suggest anyone can do accounting with their software! But buying accounting software will no more make you an accountant than buying dental equipment will make you a dentist. It's okay to drive your own car around in a city you are familiar with because you don't want to be chauffeured around. But if you *don't know how to drive* and are unfamiliar with the city, it is not okay to run out and rent a car, buy a map, and think you are going to get where you need to go! Most people don't learn to drive overnight. I'm only trying to save you and your helpers costly headaches.

Businesses come in different sizes, with different goals, in different industries, and must comply with different government regulations. But some concepts are helpful to any business. Those concepts are planning, organizing, and controlling.

Planning: The business plan is the beginning of the planning process. A one-year plan and a five-year plan are helpful. Every year, the one-year plan and five-year plans would be revised. Find a good Excel template for cash flow projections. Cash flow projections have a humbling effect. If you have created a good spreadsheet, it is easy to make changes and evaluate potential scenarios.

Organizing: The legal form of the business is *very* important. Sole proprietorship, corporation, LLC, or partnership? There are advantages and disadvantages to each. A sole proprietorship is easiest, but it leaves you open to unlimited liabilities. You can lose personal assets (like your home), even if they are not used in the business. The same risk applies to a general partner in a partnership.

I like the Sub Chapter S form of corporation since it provides legal pro-tection and opportunities to save on taxes (business and personal). That can be especially helpful if the owner or the spouse has wage income and the business experiences losses in the first few years. LLCs and PLLCs (Professional Limited Liability Corporations) are easy to form but may lose some protection across state lines (although I believe some of that is changing). Attorneys would know best. I recommend using a local attorney to set up your LLC or corporation since their prices have come down. Why not focus your efforts on business matters rather than filing incorporation documents with the state yourself?

Understand that Sub Chapter S tax treatment of your corporation or LLC is **not** automatic, even if you refer to the corporation or LLC as a *Sub S* in your state registration documents! You must apply for Sub Chapter S Corporation treatment with the **IRS** by the tenth week of the tax year you want that tax treatment to begin (March 15 for calendar year organizations). The incorporation documents and LLC filings are *state* activities, but the *IRS* grants Sub Chapter S tax filing status.

It would be a good idea to get tax advice from a professional before or during the first year of business. There are benefits to being a "C" corporation (a regular corporation). Losses of the C Corporation can be carried forward or backward to offset the corporation's income. An S corporation's net losses or net earnings are passed through to our personal income tax returns. The C Corporation allows deductions for the costs of health care plans. That deduction is not available to those with more than a 2-percent ownership of an S corporation or partnership).

A balance should be drawn between the goals of the business, the financial resources available to the business, and your personal tax profile. In other words, you want to save on taxes, but you don't want a tax-saving strategy that conflicts with the goals of the business (like health care coverage). Don't let the tax tail wag the money dog! Make money first, then be tax smart. That applies to both business and personal taxes. On the other hand, If the business is expected to suffer losses during the first couple of years and you or your spouse have significant income from other sources, losses passed through from an S Corporation, sole proprietorship, or general partnership could save some personal income taxes.

Controlling: Are the organization's financial resources adequate? How are investments in equipment or inventory to be paid for? Do you have a good relationship with a bank? Can you handle unexpected product demand? Can you expand if necessary? Are you financing the business with personal money? If so, how far do you plan to go? How far *can* you go? Work this out before you spend thousands of dollars on a business venture. You will need to have your credit in shape and your tax returns up to date if you will need financing or investors to expand. Don't expect to get ahead financially if your projected profit from the business is 10% but your financing cost is 25% from interest on credit cards you are using to run the business.

Many of the assumptions about size, direction, and financing would have been discussed in your business plan and reflected in the cash flow projections. Good planning will assist you in organizing and controlling the company.

Business can be a great activity. Small businesses can receive support and encouragement from many sources in the United States. The innovations we see in our business environment are essential to a productive, growing, and rewarding U.S. economy. Even communist countries like China and Russia have realized the benefits of profitable enterprises.

One final word. It's worth mentioning to not lay the burden of accounting on your spouse or other family member—unless you plan to hire a professional accountant to set up the accounting system for them. Financial and accounting matters can create stress even for an experienced accounting professional. Relationships can suffer greatly. Your spouse might be intrigued by this new and challenging "hobby" until it's time to pay taxes or a bank note, and there is not enough cash available because of an accounting or math mistake. The business and the relationship can go downhill from there. That's a lose-lose scenario. Friendships can be lost and never repaired.

It is important to get your business off on a good footing. Contact a good business consultant to get an idea of what will be involved before asking your family to do the bookkeeping. Once we have stable income, *where* we spend our money has implications for us all.

CHAPTER 19
Where to Shop and Invest

This might be the most challenging of subjects to undertake but we do need to consider where we spend our money. Consider spending our money a form of free speech. We want to spend it with others who believe in the democratic process, respect the Constitution, and believe we are all created equal. This is important because a lot of businesses use money to get politicians to vote their interests ahead of the public's interest. We should not spend money with corporations whose CEOs pay politicians to defeat causes we believe in (like Democracy itself). How did so much economic power wind up in the hands of so few?

Economic inequality is greater today than it was before the Great Depression. The top 10% owns 77% of America's wealth while the bottom 90% owns only 23%. (13)

So almost 300 million people (90 percent of 330 million) share only 23 percent of America's wealth! That is an astounding statistic when we consider that the U.S. has the world's largest economy, New York City is considered the financial capital of the world, and the dollar is the world's most popular currency!

Walmart and Amazon are the second and third largest employers in the United States, only the Department of Defense has more employees (counting military and civilian). Though Walmart has over a million employees, I would wager this corporation spends more on lobbying conservative politicians than they spend on employee salaries and benefits!

Amazon, for its part, has been known for so much automation that if an employee's performance measures fell below set standards, they were fired electronically—without human intervention! Amazon is currently trying to have robots deliver packages but they can't seem to handle lines in the sidewalks! It is said that their turnover is so high, in a few years, they will have run through the entire American adult population! It's a sad report on the values of American business when our second and third largest employers are thought of in such negative ways. The Department of Defense has a much better reputation, but not everyone is cut out to fly and to fight. Yet there are some businesses that value human beings and their interests.

A good organization for consumers to do business with is credit unions. Credit unions are easier to join than you might think. They want our business and have relaxed some of their requirements to affiliate. Credit unions are knowledgeable about consumer financing and consumer products and services. They can often give you better automobile financing. If you pre-arrange automobile financing with a credit union, you will be free to negotiate the automobile's selling price. With your credit union as your backstop and partner, you won't have to worry about over-paying. The credit union won't finance a car for more than its resale value.

Credit unions are also a good place to get a major credit card (Visa, Mastercard). Because they do not have a profit motive or have publicly traded stock, they are unlikely to overprice their loans. Their goals are only to help its members, protect their deposits, and break even financially. The same cannot be said about banks, especially the large banks with publicly traded stock. Many industries, including banking, spend too much money on politicians whose decisions often conflict with the financial interests of the general population.

With the Citizens United case, the Supreme Court allowed unlimited amounts of money to be spent on political campaigns. Subsequent court cases have allowed political campaigns and action groups (PACs) to hide where their money comes from. One gentleman recently gave a one-time contribution of 1.5 billion dollars (yes billion) to a republican PAC. Known for his contributions to the Federalist Society, he and they can be thanked for the current makeup of the Supreme Court.

Some companies are very open about their political activities; for instance, you have the pillow man who frequents television shows and says the 2020 election was fraudulent. As its employees fight for fair wages, Walmart fights employee union formation. Hobby Lobby, a corporation, an artificial person, went all the way to the Supreme Court (and won) to deny women employees contraception rights because that violated *its* religious beliefs! *It* is not a proper noun, so how could *it* have a spirit? Or a religion?

A good source to identify conservative corporations are conservative websites that push people to shop at conservative businesses! But understanding a company's loyalties and motivations is not as simple as we might hope.

For reference: https://www.2ndvote.com/ or Business Review Board: The Conservative's Guide for Where to Shop — The Patriot Post.

The conservative 2nd Vote group is mad with Amazon for supporting women's rights, but then Amazon has been anti-union and accused of not being employee-friendly. 2nd Vote is angry with Nike for supporting Colin Kaepernick, but what other liberal causes does Nike support? Why would 2nd Vote be angry with Walmart when Walmart is also very anti-union and has a history of paying employees very low wages? Other companies that 2nd Vote considers liberal include Target, eBay, Levi's, Best Buy, Victoria's Secret, and Nordstrom.

There is some progress. The Wall Street Journal reports Walmart is *raising* its minimum wage to twelve dollars an hour! That's $480 per week, almost $25,000 a year. (14) As the United States' second-largest employer, perhaps Walmart should consider how its low wages reflect on the perceived worth of American workers. On a positive note, Walmart should be applauded for their help on major natural disasters (hurricanes, tornados, and floods). But how much money does Walmart and the Koch Brothers give to politicians that allow energy companies to greatly contribute to global warming?

We know the Koch Industries (the Koch Brothers—only Charles remains) spends hundreds of millions of dollars a year to influence public policy in favor of energy interests as it fights climate science. David Koch was a libertarian who wanted to abolish Social Security, Medicare, the minimum wage, public transit, and other socially beneficial programs. Koch Industries has a lot of subsidiaries, including Georgia Pacific, parent of Quilted Northern tissue, Brawny paper towels, and Dixie cups. They also own Guardian Industries, a glass company, Invista, a spinoff of DuPont, and brands such as Lycra, Tactel, Thermolite, and Stainmaster.

Koch also owns Molex, an electronics company, Flint Hills Resources, and Matador Cattle Company, along with several other companies bearing the Koch name.

So where should a socially conscious person invest? Options include socially conscious mutual funds—Environmental, Social, and Corporate Governance (ESG).

The first socially conscious mutual fund family I became aware of in the 1990s was Domini (https://www.domini.com/). Domini has both stock and bond mutual funds.

Barbara Friedberg, in an article for *US News & World Report* in October 2019, wrote the following:

> The socially responsible investing category is exploding, driven by investors' desire to invest with their values. These funds are often categorized under ESG.... David Edwards, the founder of Heron Wealth, says: "This is not an easy concept to navigate, as many fund companies just slap an ESG label on an existing fund and shove it out the door." Heron adds that most socially conscious mutual funds are large-cap growth or value-focused. After excluding sectors such as carbon, tobacco or defense, the SRI mutual funds tend to overweight technology and financial services companies and subsequently are less diversified and more volatile than more broadly focused large-cap funds. To narrow

down the field (she writes), here are seven socially responsible mutual funds (15):

1. Vanguard FTSE Social Index Fund Admiral Shares
   (ticker: VFTAX);
2. Parnassus Endeavor Fund (PARWX);
3. Pax Ellevate Global Women's Leadership Fund (PXWIX);
4. Calvert Bond Fund (CSIBX);
5. Calvert International Opportunities Fund (CIOAX);
6. Fidelity U.S. Sustainability Index Fund (FITLX); and
7. Ave Maria Bond Fund (AVEFX).

Check out the prospectus information or the fund description from
their website to determine its socially conscious goals. Then check out their
historic rates of return—their profitability—to see if they may meet your
goals for investment income. Other funds I found that may have socially
conscious goals were:

VanEck Green Bond ETF (GRNB);
Jensen Quality Growth Fund Class J (JENSX);
American Funds American Mutual Fund Class F-1 (AMFFX);
MainStay Large Cap Growth Fund Class A (MLAAX); and
ClearBridge Large Cap Growth Fund Class A (SBLGX).

If you are on a tight budget or need the highest rates of return, you may
want to avoid any fund that charges high commissions (like 4–5 percent).
If you start out 5 percent in the hole because of commission expenses, the
fund will need to earn more than 11 percent to take home the stock market
average of 11 percent. In that case, you may have to stick with socially conscious funds who are also "no-load" funds.

There may be more socially conscious funds than those listed above.
I'm sure my limited research left out some worthy funds that focus on
improving our world and society. One of the drawbacks of drama-oriented

news is the lack of coverage of people and companies who do a little good every day. A lot of little good done for enough people can add up to a lot of good. The other side of investing in others is borrowing from others. There is good and bad credit as the next chapter will examine.

CHAPTER 20
Managing Credit

"If you would know the value of money, try to borrow some"
Benjamin Franklin

At the department store checkout in 2016, the clerk asked me whether I wanted to have one of their credit cards with a great introductory interest rate. I thought for a second and replied, "No, actually, I would like to loan the department store some money so that I could earn some interest!" When we don't have enough income to make ends meet, we can develop a mindset that borrowing money is a normal state of affairs. It may be normal in times of stagnant wages and rising costs, but it is not good to owe when we are trying to become financially independent. We especially don't want to use department store credit cards that are notorious for high-interest rates.

The only consumer credit purchases we should carry balances on are for our homes and cars. For most people, it is difficult to pay cash for a car or home. If we choose to pay cash for the car, we should get it for much less than the asking price. If you can pay cash for a house, you are in a different league than 99 percent of us. When we do need to purchase necessities on credit, we should try to get the lowest interest rates. The lower the interest rate, the less we pay in total. To get the lowest interest rates, we need to have good credit.

To create and maintain a good credit rating, it is best to get a major credit card (Visa, Mastercard) through your bank or credit union. Pay balances off monthly if you can. Paying a lot of interest expense does **not** improve our credit score. Making small purchases that you can pay off monthly is a good way to create good credit history. A good tool to use to plan your way out of debt is "Power Pay" (https://powerpay.org/). We focus on reducing debt in the next chapter.

Some vendors, such as home improvement companies and medical providers, issue credit cards and charge no interest–if paid off within a certain time period (one to two years). These contracts can help you establish a good payment history. But be careful how the vendors price their goods or services. Also, be careful that you don't miss a payment and do pay it off within the agreed-upon time, or the no-interest provision will be lost. That is especially important if you are trying to establish a good payment history.

A Final caution: Verify the period of time to receive the no-interest terms. Suppose at the time of sale your agreement was that you have two years to pay off the purchase interest-free. But their billing system has coded you with only six months to pay the balance off interest-free! You could have a fight over a significant amount of accrued interest two years from now. You must straighten things out now while it is fresh on everyone's minds! You don't want to have to pay dearly for the company's mistake.

Another factor that affects your credit score is your percentage of credit used. Try and keep it to less than 33 percent. So if you have a $6,100 line of credit, don't exceed $2,013. Limit it to 30% to be more conservative.

Your *credit to income* ratio is also a factor that affects your credit score. It is an indication of your ability to pay. If your income is $40,000 per year, it doesn't look good if you have consumer debt of $45,000.

Try and limit inquires on your credit. It's best to have all your credit inquiries occur within the same fifteen days (and limit that practice to once or twice a year). So if you are planning to buy a car, apply for a home equity loan or refinancing, or apply for a credit card—try and apply for them all within the same fifteen-day period.

It's worth repeating, paying a lot of interest (finance charges) does not improve your credit score. Using good credit like a major credit card, keeping low balances, and paying consistently will. Once we have used the credit, we need to be smart about paying off the balances.

CHAPTER 21

Effective Ways to Reduce Debt

He who builds his house with credit does so on unstable ground

I understand the spirit of the words above but buying a home or car on credit is good use of credit—especially if you can get good interest rates. It's the other consumer debt and our total amount of debt we need to be careful with. With stagnant wages over the past fifty years and banks behind the proliferation of credit cards, we should not be surprised that so many people are mired in debt. It's worth mentioning that the banks also lobbied Congress to revise the bankruptcy law in 2005, making it more difficult for individuals to discharge debts.

There are four effective approaches we can take to get out of debt:

A. Pay more towards the debts with the higher interest rates
B. Use PowerPay to help manage our payments and schedules ([https:// powerpay.org/](https://powerpay.org/))
C. Consult a credit counselor to help with a plan
D. Consolidate your debts with a lower interest rate creditor, but be careful of any transfer fees (I usually don't recommend this); and
E. As a last resort, bankruptcy may be an option, but a credit counselor will have to be involved.

Paying more toward the debts with the higher interest rates is an effective way to reduce debts. Just be sure you don't miss the minimum payments to other creditors, and that the total payments fit within your budget.

The PowerPay tool is beneficial in helping you see a light at the end of the tunnel. You input your information into worksheets, and you will be able to see where your balances will be at certain points in time, and when the debts will be paid off.

Because of the compounding effect of interest, there is the chance that you will not be able to pay off your balances in a reasonable period of time. That's when you will need professional help. For instance, let's say you owe creditors a total of $50,000, and your *average* interest rate is 15 percent. Tools like PowerPay, or an on-line financial calculator could help you calculate the amount of the monthly payments and how long it would take to pay it off. With those two factors, you would have to make payments of at least $807 per month for ten years to pay off the $50,000 balance. If you cannot pay the calculated amount per month consistently for ten years and have no options to reduce the interest rates, you should seek guidance from a credit counselor.

A credit counselor may be able to get creditors to jointly agree to lesser balances or lower interest rates. Many counselors are non-profit, but I would still research their reputation on the web and look for reviews. In helping military members, I found reliable assistance with the National Foundation for Credit Counseling (http://www.nfcc.org/).

Some other things you can do:

Complete a personal financial inventory. Tracing how you got into debt might help you find the right solutions to get out. It's good to know what you own, what you owe, and how much you're spending.

Put away the plastic. If you find yourself over your head in debt, stop using your credit cards immediately.

Call your creditors before skipping payments. If you think you can't make a payment, call the company you owe and ask for more time.

Mail your payments early. When paying your credit card by mail, send your payment several days before the due date (at least a week). This is very important. Credit card companies typically require that payments are posted to your account by a certain time of day on your due date, or they will charge you a late fee. You can avoid fees by paying online. Set up an automatic (scheduled) payment for the amount you can regularly pay monthly.

Avoid settlement or credit repair scams. There is no easy fix to getting out of debt or repairing a bad credit record. Stay away from services that require up-front fees or "voluntary contributions." Avoid those who guarantee they can make your debts go away or promise you will pay only pennies on the dollar.

Join a credit union. Credit unions are great places to learn about consumer finance and consumer products. Their interest rates will be reasonable too.

Consider bankruptcy as a last resort. Some people think bankruptcy is the only option when their debts become too much to manage. The credit counselor will guide you through this option. In fact, getting credit counseling is now a requirement to file bankruptcy under the bankruptcy law passed in 2005.

I've seen many people turn their financial lives around, but it takes initiative and motivation. Find yours by thinking of the things you want and need. Keep open communication with the people trying to help you. One day soon, you will be able to reward them with guidance and kindness of your own. Student loans are a debt that affects millions of Americans.

CHAPTER 22
Paying Back Student Loans

Knowledge should not be so expensive that we choose to be stupid.

At the time of this writing, student loans are a significant burden to millions of Americans. Estimates in 2020 put outstanding student loan debt at about 1.6 trillion dollars (16). So it's important to discuss some of the major concerns in dealing with student loan debt:

1. *Warning*: Parents should beware of signing a Parent Plus loan because they will have few or no options to eliminate this debt if the student doesn't pay it. The government could even attach a parent's social security check to repay a Parent Plus loan! Students, please do not bring this type of agreement home for your parents to sign. It would be better to arrange other sources of financial aid.

2. **In August 2022 President Biden announced cancellation of up to $10,000 of student loan debt for individual borrowers with incomes of less than $125,000 per year. The Administration would cancel up to $20,000 of a student's loan debt if the student received Pell Grants.**

3. Student loans generally are not dischargeable in bankruptcy. So it can be a burden, even during the worst of times.

4. There are four income-based student loan repayment plans. One or two of them will be more favorable for your situation than the others. Learn which ones you qualify for from your loan servicer.

5. Public Service Loan Forgiveness (PSLF) is an option to have student loan balances forgiven. After working ten years for the government, military, or selected non-profit organizations and consistently paying on the loan, any remaining loan balance could be forgiven.

6. The Teacher Loan Forgiveness Program is also an option. Under the Teacher Loan Forgiveness Program, if you teach full-time for five complete and consecutive academic years in a low-income school or educational service agency, you may be eligible for forgiveness of up to $17,500 on your Direct Subsidized and Unsubsidized Loans and your Subsidized and Unsubsidized Federal Stafford Loans (US Department of Education 2000).

The income-based repayment plans are tied to the US Poverty Guidelines–US Department of Health & Human Services 2020, (17) and the monthly payment required to pay the loan off over a ten-year period. Consider how your payments in the future might be affected under each of the four income-based repayment plans available (18). Here are some provisions of each:

a. Repay Plan:
   i. The government pays a lot of your interest on *both* subsidized and unsubsidized loans;
   ii. Your future payments could exceed the ten-year payment plan if your income increases;
   iii. Spouse's income is considered unless practically legally separated;
   iv. Probably better when there is significant unsubsidized debt; and
   v. Interest can be added for failing to recertify or voluntarily leaving the plan.
b. Pay Plan:
   i. Government pays the interest on subsidized loans for first three years;

ii. Future payments will *never* exceed the monthly payment of the ten-year plan;

iii. Spouse's income may be excluded if filing separate tax returns;

iv. Interest (up to 10 percent of loan) can be added if no longer qualified or voluntarily leaving plan; and

v. Consider the amount of additional income taxes before filing separate tax returns.

c. IBR Plan (Available to FFEL and Direct Loan Borrowers):

i. Government pays the interest on subsidized loans for first three years;

ii. Future payments will *never* exceed the monthly payment of the ten-year plan;

iii. Spouse's income may be excluded if filing separate tax returns;

iv. "Unlimited" interest can be added if no longer qualified or voluntarily leaving plan; and

v. Consider the amount of additional income taxes before filing separate tax returns.

d. ICR Plan:

i. Government pays **no** interest on loans;

ii. Your future payments "could" exceed the monthly payment of the ten-year plan if your income increases;

iii. Spouse's income may be excluded if filing a separate tax return;

iv. Interest (up to 10 percent of loan) can be added "annually" if no longer qualified or voluntarily leaving plan; and

v. Consider the amount of additional income taxes before filing separate tax returns.

The information above is provided in more detail from the US Department of Education (Federal Student Aid; US Department of Education 2020). You can find several references with guidance on how to decide which repayment plan is best for you (US Department of Education 2000) (19).

Before you decide which of the above plans would be best for you, it would be best to check with your loan servicer to see which ones you qualify for. Considering that loans can be subsidized or unsubsidized, and direct or indirect, you virtually need computer software to determine which repayment plans you qualify for, and you could still come to the wrong conclusion! So let the loan servicer determine which ones you qualify for since they would have to be in agreement anyway.

The loan servicer may want to recommend the type of loan repayment plan they feel is best for you. Discuss the matter and see if you agree with their reasoning. It may be worth seeking an independent financial professional's opinion before agreeing with a repayment plan you have reservations about.

If you intend to use the Public Service Loan Forgiveness program after working for the government (or non-profit) and paying consistently for ten years, I have three recommendations: (1) Go to the StudentAid.gov website and ensure that your agency or organization is one of the approved organizations; (2) keep your W-2 forms and tax returns to prove you worked for the organization(s) over the years (this is especially important for smaller organizations that might not be around for ten years); and (3) don't leave or retire from the organization until after you have submitted your application for loan forgiveness (you may even want to wait until it has been approved before leaving).

If you are considering Active military service, some military branches may pay off some or all of your student loans for accepting assignments in critical career fields. The Army does this for many assigned to the medical field. Like student loan debt, significant tax debt can also be a burden.

CHAPTER 23

Offers in Compromise

Asking the IRS to Accept Less Than You Owe

This information about the Offer in Compromise (OIC) is provided to give you some perspective about the process and what's involved. If you feel you owe the IRS too much to pay your balance owed in a reasonable time period, you should seek professional help to with filing an OIC. Shop around for pricing and referrals before deciding to prepare an offer yourself.

Many consulting companies will prepare Offers in Compromise to the IRS. While many television ads suggest certainty of debt forgiveness, it is up to the IRS to determine whether your situation is dire enough and your offer is high enough, that they will accept your offer. Because preparation fees can be high, consulting companies often require that you owe at least $10,000 before preparing an OIC for you.

There is no magic to the process of filing an OIC, but your income and allowable expenses need to show that you are not in a position to pay more than you are offering. Basically, you are showing the IRS your financial situation is so difficult that it is in their interest to accept your offer. You are saying your financial situation is bad, not expected to improve, or may even get worse. A good time to prepare an OIC is when you are out of work, your earnings have decreased, or there has been a medical condition or other circumstance that significantly impacts your finances.

Whether you prepare the offer yourself or use a professional, understand that it is a negotiation. Make your offer in good faith and expect a good-faith response from the IRS.

The offer is made on Treasury Form 656. The Offer in Compromise Booklet for Form 656 will provide instructions. Be sure to include all of the tax periods and types of taxes that you owe when you file your offer. You are allowed to borrow the amount you are offering. You can even put down 20 percent of your offer and after approval, pay the balance off over a five-month period.

Your reason for the offer: This is where you will need to explain the circumstances that caused your financial difficulties and prevents you from paying the balance of your taxes owed.

You will also need to complete Form 433-A to list your assets, liabilities, and monthly income and expenses. Be sure to include all expenses, including any taxes being withheld from your salary for current taxes. Form 433-A is also used to for sole-proprietorship businesses.

If you have a corporation, partnership, or LLC you will need to complete Form 433B. If you are in business and want to file an OIC, I strongly recommend obtaining professional assistance.

An offer in compromise can work for you if your financial situation has been severely compromised and you do not see an opportunity for improvement in the near future. OICs are successful when your situation is bad and you explain it properly — not because the consultant has some special relationship with the IRS. If your earnings have not diminished, and there has not been a significant disruptive incident in your life, an OIC may not be successful. The acceptance of an OIC may relieve you of some overwhelming tax burdens. If you are sixty-two or older and a homeowner, you may be able to improve your standard of living with a reverse mortgage.

CHAPTER 24
Reverse Mortgages (Pros and Cons)

However you feel about TV celebrities advertising, closer analysis is required to determine whether or not they are promoting a good product. Luckily, we have academic studies showing that reverse mortgages can be helpful in many circumstances. A reverse mortgage, also known as a Home Equity Conversion Mortgage (HECM), can be a good source of money for senior citizen homeowners (sixty-two and older).

If re-financing your mortgage would lower your monthly mortgage payment to your satisfaction that might be a better option than a HECM. It depends upon the expected interest rate, how much you need, and your goal for the money. With a HECM you can usually borrow 30 to 80 percent of the equity in your home. A line of credit with a HECM can also provide funds for long-term care.

The HECM can allow you to wait longer to draw your social security. It can also be used if you want to preserve your stock portfolio when the stock market is down (like most of 2022). University studies show that with good use of the HECM, your portfolio of investments will last longer, and your social security benefits will be higher. Each year you wait to draw your social security, your benefit increases between 7 and 8 percent per year (you get the maximum benefit at age seventy). That's the equivalent of **59 percent** more social security per month by waiting from age sixty-two until age seventy (just be sure your health will permit you to live beyond age 80).

A HECM is better than a Home Equity Line of Credit (HELOC) because the period allowed to draw on the HELOC may end, the principal payback period for the HELOC may be shorter, and the payment amount may be higher. The bank could also "freeze" a HELOC or cancel it at their whim. The Reverse Mortgage line of credit enables you to deal with inflation regardless of whether the home value increases or decreases. Here are some facts:

Until the last participant in the home dies, moves, or sells the home:

+ You never have to make a payment (unless you want to);
+ You will never owe more than the value of the house;
+ You never have to give up title to the home; and
+ You will never have to move.

In circumstances of divorce, where the home is sold, each spouse can get equivalent housing without obtaining more mortgage debt. If one spouse remains in the home, the other spouse can buy them out with a HECM, and they can both live in houses of equal value with neither having a mortgage.

There may be three downsides with reverse mortgages (assess for yourself if they are deal breakers):

1. The reverse mortgage will occupy the first lien position, so that makes it difficult to borrow more money using the house as collateral once the reverse mortgage is executed;
2. The homeowner's beneficiaries will inherit a home with less equity. So a parent needs to weigh the impact of the HECM on the children or others who would inherit the house. Will the children want to live in the home, or will they want to sell it for the equity they inherit? If the heirs want to live in the home, how much of a mortgage would be left? And would the heirs qualify for a mortgage and be able to make the payments? Unless the homeowner makes payments against the reverse mortgage, the balance owed will increase. The residual debt from the HECM could possibly be addressed by carrying sufficient life insurance on the parent/

homeowner. These considerations should be worked out ahead of taking out a HECM;

3. Reverse mortgages do have fees. There is a loan origination fee and mortgage insurance premium. There is a margin that adds 1–3 percent to the interest rate. Get an understanding of these fees and have the reverse mortgage representative project their cost. Then consider it in relation to the HECM's benefit to you.

Although reverse mortgages retain a first lien position, if the home increases significantly in value, the reverse mortgage can be re-financed.

As with all matters dealing with money, consider the pros and cons. If the additional cost of the reverse mortgage is still more attractive than other financial options, go for it. If the reverse mortgage can provide you needed capital until your long-term investments rebound and their potential growth exceeds the HECM fees, it is probably a good choice. If the reverse mortgage allows you to postpone taking social security, and the growth in your social security benefits far exceed the HECM fees, it would be a good choice. See *the chapter on social security for more discussion of when best to take social security benefits.*

Finally, home values ordinarily increase at a rate higher than inflation, and that will help offset the impact of the HECM on the equity the heirs will inherit. Having adequate life insurance and a burial policy will assist your beneficiaries greatly. Beneficiaries and heirs are prominent in the next topic, estate planning.

CHAPTER 25
Estate Planning (Survivorship Planning, Avoiding Probate)

I'm always amused after listening to a good financial planning program where 50 percent of the discussion involved income taxes, and the program ends with, "This program was not meant to provide tax advice; please see your tax advisor for guidance on taxes!" I know the attorneys are just trying to protect the radio program, but when it comes to estate planning, I say genuinely, "*Please consult an attorney for help with your estate plan.*" That is because the consequences of getting it wrong can be of great cost to you and your loved ones.

The goal of this chapter is only to provide you with knowledge of some of the matters to consider in estate planning. If your estate is not subject to federal estate taxes, you may be able to use an attorney who doesn't specialize in estate planning and simply have a will or trust prepared. That might be adequate to have your property transferred according to your wishes.

Estates (property transferred at death) are not taxed at the federal level unless your taxable estate exceeds 12 million dollars for an individual or 24 million dollars for couples. But even someone with moderate assets or real property should be concerned with how their assets will be transferred to heirs when they pass away. We want to avoid having the state transfer titles. The state's title transfer process is called probate).

The transfer of title to property upon death can be accomplished by law, contract (trust or beneficiary designation), Will, or the probate process.

The hierarchy by which title to property transferred is:

1. By Law, for instance, real estate. If there is a statute involved, the statute takes precedence.
2. By Contract. For instance, a life insurance policy or investment product that designates a beneficiary—Payable on Death, POD instruction.
3. By Will. The Will states who will receive which property upon the testator's death. The executor must have the surrogate court "stamp" the will and then carry out its instructions. If there is no Will, the property must be transferred by probate.

Property not transferred by contract or will might be transferred by law (number 1 above). The law is superior to the other forms of transfer. The law applies when there is a joint owner and right of survivorship of assets exists. Joint owners could include a spouse (tenants by the entirety). Some states have laws that do not allow disinheriting a spouse (i.e. the spouse might be entitled to one-third of the estate, no matter what was in the will).

Title or ownership of some property can be passed by *contract* and are superior to claims of a will or trust. These transfer on death documents (TOD) include the beneficiary designations on bank accounts, life insurance, or investments like IRAs or 401ks. If you re-marry and want your current spouse to inherit the investments, you will need to *update* your beneficiary form. Listing in your will that the property will go to your current spouse will **not** override the beneficiary designation form. Transfer of title can also be done by trust.

A *revocable* or *living* trust is a vehicle where the title to the property only becomes effective upon your death. You could put your home, car, investments, or other property into a revocable trust so that the title is transferred when you pass. Know that the trust must actually be *funded* with the property after the trust is created. Since the trust is revocable, you can change it at any time. An attorney can provide specific details. Some states have relaxed the requirements for real estate or automobiles to be trans-ferred upon death by simply completing a form (trust not required). *But it's important to verify with the state that they have, in fact, filed and recorded your completed form.*

A trust allows long-term control over the distribution of the property in the trust. Not only does it avoid probate but it is also good for multi-gen-erational planning. You don't need to bring the trust document to a surro-gate court as you must do with a Will. Your trustee acts as your agent and carries out your instructions.

Property not required to be transferred by law, trust, or transfer on death documents, that can be transferred using a Will include cash, art, or jewelry. The scope of properties today might even include digital assets. You may have produced some valuable social media. If so, heirs will need access to social media accounts and passwords.

The thorniest process for transferring title to successors is probate. When property is orphaned (you die and no one has the title to your prop-erty), the state will decide who will get the title, based upon the laws of the state. Taxes, claims, and debts are paid, and a process is followed to decide how the residual of properties are distributed among successors. Depending upon your state of residence, your spouse is first; if they are deceased, then to your children; if no children, then to your parents. The process may take a full year or more to accomplish.

You may also have a need to create powers of attorney (POAs). They appoint agents to conduct certain matters on your behalf. The following are types of POAs you can create:

General – The appointed can do everything for you;

Special – Limited, for instance, authority to sell your car;

Durable – Survives your incapacity—if you are incapable of con-ducting your affairs;

Health Care – Gives someone the power to make decisions about your medical care; and

Springing – Takes effect after an event—after you are incapacitated (but your agent's hands could be tied up trying to get two doctors to say you are incapacitated).

The Durable Power of Attorney might give your agent the most flexibility. Some attorneys recommend there be an end date of one or two years out. Entities will often be suspect of "stale" (old) powers of attorneys, which could slow down your agent's performance.

In addition to a will, you may also want to have an *Advance Will Directive*—a living will. This complements a health care power of attorney. The living will would include your "end of life" instructions. For instance, "Keep me on a ventilator for at least two months or give me pain medication if required."

There are many risks in leaving assets to be transferred by the probate process. For one thing, the state charges a fee. Also, any wishes you may have had for the distribution of your assets will not be considered. The probate process, or even a poorly drafted trust or will, could result in ill feelings among successors.

Of great concern are transfers among blended families. Without proper provisions in a residuary or contingent trust, your children might not see any of your assets. For instance, if your children's step-father inherits your property, remarries, and he dies and leaves everything to his new spouse, your children will have no claim on what you left to their step-father (your surviving spouse). This risk might also be addressed with a *pre-nuptial* or *post-nuptial* agreement.

Getting organized: Many experts recommend creating a "Grab Bag" or "Go-to Book" for important documents. The grab bag could include things like:

Types of medicines (and dosages);
Allergies;
Copies of insurance cards;
Doctors and phone numbers;

Powers of Attorney; and

Advance Medical Directives.

Copies of documents could be stored in a fire-proof safe with the key or combination shared with a trusted person. Documents could be scanned to a file and put on a thumb drive. I suppose an on-line location in the 'cloud' is an option but I would be concerned about security. At a minimum, a trusted person (perhaps a younger relative) should know where important documents are and how to access them.

In graduate school, I took a course in estate planning. I must have been halfway through the course when I came to realize the object of the course was to lower taxes on estates of over 1.5 million dollars. I think a better title for the course would have been Estate *Tax* Planning. At that time, 1982, the highest tax rate on estates was about 55 percent, and that applied to taxable assets above about 1.5 million. With such a high tax rate on a low taxable threshold, planning to avoid estate taxes made sense.

Fast forward to 2021, the first $11.7 million of a person's assets is exempt from federal estate taxes. For couples, the first 23.5 million are exempt and the highest tax rate is down to 40 percent. If you are at risk of estate tax, you can reduce your estate by giving away up to $15,000 per year to any number of people, related to you or not. An estate planning attorney can design strategies to transfer your assets to your successors to avoid the tax.

There are several estate planning techniques available to reduce your estate tax: the marital deduction, A&B Trusts, QTIP Trusts, and life-time gifts. Also, life insurance proceeds can be exempted from taxation if set up properly (Crummy Power Trusts). Any residual estate tax could be paid from life insurance proceeds. Less than one-tenth of 1 percent of Americans will have these concerns.

In light of these high thresholds and the many options to avoid estate taxes, why are so many in Congress and the financial services industry still agonizing over estate taxes? The Brookings Institute estimates about 4,000 estate tax returns are filed in a year and only about 1,900 will be taxable.

(20) Those legislators who fight so diligently to minimize the tax liabilities of the top one-tenth of 1 percent might put a little effort into improving the lives of the other 330 million Americans. However current campaign financing laws provide them no incentive to do that.

As mentioned above, this discussion is not a substitute for estate planning. There are many aspects of estate planning other than reducing estate taxes. My goals were simply to discuss some of the components and aspects of it. For additional guidance you may also want to visit:

Estate Planning for the Servicemember—YouTube/
https://www.youtube.com/watch?feature=youtu.
be&v=7WmIzSmXeew&app=desktop/

CHAPTER 26
Cryptocurrency

C ryptocurrency came on the scene in 2009, getting a great deal of market attention in 2013. Bitcoin, the dominant cryptocurrency, was introduced by a computer programmer, Satoshi Nakamoto. He published a white paper sending it to a number of cryptographers on October 31, 2008. It was entitled "Bitcoin: A Peer-to-Peer Electronic Cash System" (21). The software was released in January 2009 and the first Bitcoin was minted.

The results of a 2022 survey conducted by Bitwise Investments entitled "The Bitwise/ETF Trends 2022 Benchmark Survey of Financial Advisor Attitudes Toward Crypto Assets" found that almost ½ of financial advisors have some crypto assets in their personal portfolio of investments. The survey also found that among advisors allocating crypto to client accounts, 80% held crypto up to 5% in their client's portfolios. (21)

It is difficult to analyze the complex cloud of information surrounding cryptocurrencies. Adding to the confusion is the highly technical nature of these assets. Without some training in computer science, it is difficult to discuss cryptocurrencies and their purpose. It will be helpful to define the following terms:

Block – Data structures within a blockchain, a place where information is stored.

Blockchain – A distributed ledger of verified transactions or information (a group of blocks)

Cryptocurrency – A digital asset, a medium of exchange that relies on cryptography (i.e., blockchain).

Miners – Nodes (computers) competing to add blocks to the blockchain by solving a mathematical puzzle (for a reward and possibly transaction fees).

Decentralized and Distributed Database – An updated, verified blockchain (ledger) that all participating miners (computers) have access to.

Non-Fungible Tokens (NFTs) – a financial security consisting of digital data stored in a blockchain. They can represent real objects like art or music. They generally have unique, identifying codes and are sold for digital currency.

Satoshi – 100,000,000 Satoshis equals one Bitcoin (used because of Bitcoin's high price)

Nakamoto 's 'peer-to-peer' cash system was designed to go around the banks and move money (digital assets) from sender to receiver in less time. The receiver's bank would no longer have to wait until it was sure the sender had adequate funds in his or her account before providing payment to the recipient.

With crypto's distributed ledger feature, all participating computers would see the same updated and verified ledger (the blockchain) in real time. The only time delay to send money would be the time it takes computers to solve the next blocks—the best solution, completing the blockchain, and updating the ledger.

At the time of this writing, Bitcoin pays 6.25 Bitcoins in reward to the miner (computer) that comes up with the best block (the best and fastest way to get the money from a particular sender to a particular receiver). The reward can be significant, motivating thousands of miners (computers) around the world to compete. The sender may also provide a separate fee to motivate miners to engage in solving the puzzle.

There have been complaints about hidden fees when using cryptocurrency. That may be the fee that the sender offers for their transaction to be solved and settled. Supposedly, if you don't offer a fee, the miners have less incentive to create solutions and the necessary blocks. So if you don't propose a fee, the solution for your transaction would have to wait until there was less activity (or you agree to pay the necessary fee to have your transaction finalized). The fee (paid in Bitcoin) is subtracted from your remaining Bitcoin balance.

According to Bitcoin and others who study cryptocurrency, we can have great trust in the validity of the finalized blockchain. No blockchain is finalized without at least six added blocks (from six computers) each scrutinizing the previous block. Hacking is virtually non-existent because of verification procedures such as hash functions and digital signatures. Each user and sender have public keys and private keys to access transactions. (Just watch out for fraudulent crypto apps when initially investing in crypto!)

Because only you have your private key code it is imperative that you do not lose it! Without your private key code, you can say goodbye to your investment! As far as the cryptocurrency is concerned, you no longer exist! Non-Fungible Tokens (NFTs) also rely on blockchain for validation.

NFTs, Non-Fungible Tokens can represent everything from fine art to theater tickets. NFTs can be minted or created for intangible, tangible, or digital objects or any combination of the three. Often the NFT is created from existing images or videos freely available to the public. But once you create an NFT it has your unique blockchain (authentication) and you can sell it for whatever the market will bear. Note some outrageous prices have been paid for works that a smart teenager could have put together between their math and English homework assignments.

So how do you determine the value of computer generated blockchains or the value of an NFT? This gets to the crux of the dilemma with cryptocurrencies and NFTs. If the value is only determined by what people are willing to pay, beware, public interest can diminish overnight!

One can find a price for just about anything available for sale, but to know *value*, which is superior to price, more scrutiny is required. Value is determined by the demand, urgency of need, utility, and scarcity of an item. Because cryptocurrencies are so new to the marketplace, it's very difficult to determine their value.

Let's spend a minute discussing what the top ten cryptocurrencies are supposed to do. Decide for yourself whether their mission or vision is realistic and what value that might be to society or the marketplace.

We know Bitcoin's mission is to send money faster (faster than the banks)

Ethereum's vision is: To create a world computer that anyone can build applications on in a decentralized manner.

Tether: Tether is a stablecoin pegged to the US Dollar. (A stablecoin is a type of cryptocurrency whose value is pegged to another fiat currency).

USD Coin: A fully collateralized US dollar stablecoin. USDC is the bridge between dollars and trading on cryptocurrency exchanges.

BNB: Binance Coin (BNB) is an exchange-based token created and issued by the Binance Cryptocurrency Exchange.

XRP (Ripple – Fred Sandford's drink?) Ripple is a privately-held fintech company that provides a global payment solution via its patented payment network called Ripple Network (also known as RippleNet) (Sounds like some competition for Bitcoin?)

Binance USD: A stable coin pegged to USD that has received approval from the New York State Department of Financial Services (NYDFS).

Cardano: A decentralized platform that will allow complex programmable transfers of value in a secure and scalable fashion. The Cardano project is different from other blockchain projects as it openly addresses the need for regulatory oversight while maintaining consumer privacy and protections through an innovative software architecture.

Solana: A high throughput blockchain based on the Proof of History (PoH) and Proof of Stake (PoS) consensus. Built by a team of networking engineers, Solana aims to become the blockchain infrastructure for modern internet applications.

Dogecoin: Created as a fun cryptocurrency that will appeal beyond the core Bitcoin audience. Dogecoin is primarily used as a tipping system on Reddit and Twitter where users tip each other for creating or sharing good content. The community is very active in organizing fundraising activities for deserving causes.

Is it just me or do these cryptocurrencies seem tied to each other's technology or target markets? Even though Cardano and Solana seem to have a vision for their role in future marketplaces, how can you put a value on their utility at this point in time? Until the average investor can figure out a true value for these alternative currencies, it is very risky to invest in them. Perhaps after government regulations are implemented and the cost of creating and maintaining them become more expensive, the flood of cryptocurrencies will diminish and there will be less piggyback and piling on. If there were fewer cryptocurrencies operating in fewer lanes, perhaps we might be able to appreciate their value. Maybe then we can take a more serious look.

Dogecoin (the currency of K-9s?) does seem to separate itself from the crowd by attempting to address deserving causes. Odd that it was originally introduced as a 'joke' currency!

I will say that there may be some utility for NFTs, for instance in authenticating concert tickets more easily, protecting rights of creative artists, and validating ownership of items. I am more positive we can reach price/value equilibrium for *some* NFTs than I am that the market can properly value cryptocurrencies.

The challenge we face in valuing crypto is cutting through all the hype with which these alternative assets are promoted. We are faced with a ton of information and new concepts when it comes to cryptocurrency. And if you read the material put out by the crypto marketeers (Bitcoin, Ethereum, XRP and others) crypto is the best thing since sliced bread and a must for all investors! A major celebrity was fined 1.3 million dollars by the SEC in October 2022 for promoting a cryptocurrency without disclosing that she was being paid to promote the cryptocurrency!

By January 2022 there were more than 9,900 cryptocurrencies. New tokens are popping up all the time – each with a different use and backstory. (22) Even some governments are embracing cryptocurrencies, and businesses of all types are trying to incorporate them into their business models. The proponents with interests in these alternative currencies open their essays with comments like, "crypto is here to stay". They suggest 'blockchain' technologies will replace authentication services, perhaps replacing notaries and other respected professionals.

But looming on the horizon is the impact of impending government regulations. How will the U.S. Government (Executive Branch, Congress, and possibly the courts) respond with laws and regulation of cryptocurrencies? The President, in an Executive Order issued March 9, 2022, is requiring some *20* federal agencies to provide comment by October 2022 on the potential consequences of cryptocurrency. (23) These federal agencies are required to coordinate and address concerns like global financial stability, illicit financial risks such as money laundering, cybercrime and ransomware, narcotics and human trafficking, and terrorism and proliferation financing! (23) (allegedly, many nefarious behaviors were engaged in and paid for using crypto).

Many people may be attracted by the fact that there is currently so little government regulation. They may like the fact that there is no censorship or permission required to participate in the crypto market. What information can we use to help us gain some perspective on the pricing of cryptocurrencies?

I decided to use an old-fashioned approach to evaluate the potential market value or price of cryptocurrencies: Let's look at the performances of the top ten, leading cryptocurrencies and isolate important facts and trends. The source of the following information is from the website: coingecko.com, July 14, 2022. (24) Due to the high volatility of crypto, I recommend you visit this site or other sites like coinmarketcap.com to get updated price information. No doubt the prices will have changed by the time this book is printed!

The number one crypto in terms of market dominance was Bitcoin with about 41% of the market. Bitcoin's price in July 2022 was about $20,000, down about 72% from its all-time high of about $69,000 in November 2021. Its lowest price was about $68 in July 2013. Its circulating supply was about 19 million while its maximum supply and total supply were 21 million. Bitcoin's proponents say that limiting the maximum supply of Bitcoin will have a positive impact on its price. The theory is that prices increase for things that are in limited supply. But don't pull out your checkbook yet!

Following Bitcoin in the number two position in terms of market dominance is Ethereum with about 14% of the market. Ethereum's price in July 2022 was about $1,077, down about 78% from its all-time high of about $4,878 in November 2021. Its lowest price was about 43 cents in October 2015. Its circulating supply was around 120 million and its total supply was also about 120 million. It did not have a maximum supply number.

Coming in the third position was Tether with about 7% of the market. Tether's price in July 2022 was about $1.00, down about 24% from its all-time high of about $1.32 in July 2018. Its lowest price was about 57 cents in March 2015. Its circulating supply was around 66 billion and its total supply was also about 66 billion. It also did not have a maximum supply number.

Running in the fourth position in terms of market dominance was USD Coin with about 6% of the market. USD Coin's price in July 2022 was about $1.00, down about 15% from its all-time high of about $1.17 in May 2019. Its lowest price was about 90 cents in May 2021.Its circulating supply was around 55 billion and its total supply was also about 55 billion. It did not have a maximum supply number.

In fifth place in terms of market dominance is BND with about 4% of the market. BND's price in July 2022 was about $226, down about 67% from its all-time high of about $686 in May 2021. Its lowest price was about 4 cents in October 2017. It's circulating supply and total supply was about 163 million while its *maximum* supply was about 165 million.

Bitcoin and BND both have higher prices and they both fixed the maximum supply of coins. They are both also down about 70% from their highs in 2021. Is that coincidental? Looks like 2021 was the year that cryptos reached their peak in price. It doesn't look like limiting the maximum supply of a cryptocurrency provides any upward support to its price.

In the sixth position in market dominance in the crypto market was Binance USD with about 2% of the market. Binance USD's price in July 2022 was about $1.00, down about 13% from its all-time high of about

$1.15 in March of 2020. Its lowest price was about 90 cents May 2021. Its circulating supply was around 18 billion and its total supply was also about 18 billion. It did not have a maximum supply number.

Running in seventh place in terms of market dominance was XRP with a bit less than 2% of the market. XRP's price in July 2022 was about 31 cents, down about 91% from its all-time high of about $3.40 in January 2018. Its lowest price was less than *one* cent May 2014. Its circulating supply was about 48 billion and total supply was about 99,989,535,142 (almost 100 billion) while its *maximum* supply was 100 billion.

In spite of the comments by supporters of Bitcoin that controlling the maximum supply has an upward push on price, I see just the opposite! At least three cryptocurrencies with significant drops in price among the top 10 each had a maximum on their supply of coin!

Rounding the curve in eighth position was Cardano with less than 2% of the market. Cardano's price in July 2022 was about 43 cents, down about 86% from its all-time high of about $3.09 in September 2021. Its lowest price was about 2 cents in March of 2020. Its circulating supply was around 34 billion and its total supply and maximum supply were 45 billion.

In the ninth position in market dominance was Solana with less than 1% of the market. Solana's price in July 2022 was about $34.50, down almost 87% from its all-time high of about $260.00 in November 2021. Its lowest price was about 50 cents in May 2020. Its circulating supply was around 350 million and its total supply was about 510 million. It did not have a maximum supply number.

In the tenth position in market dominance in the crypto market was Dogecoin with less than 1% of the market. Dogecoin's price in July 2022 was about six cents, down about 92% from its all-time high of about 73 cents in May 2021. Its lowest price was less than one cent in May 2015. Its circulating supply was around 132.5 billion. No total supply or maximum supply numbers were reported. (Dogecoin was moved to 11th place by August 2022 beaten out by Polkadot).

Discussion: We can see that by mid-2021 cryptocurrencies began to drop significantly in price and that continued into 2022. Was the record high in early 2021 due to the Coronavirus pandemic taking such a toll on our lives in 2020? (i.e. were people making irrational bets or looking for new ways to connect?) Then was the sharp drop in prices in 2021 a response to the record high inflation? Did people raid their crypto for additional funds to deal with higher inflation? Or did they begin to feel that crypto was overpriced and tried to cut their losses?

Whatever the reasons for the significant drops in crypto prices in 2021, investments that experience such great drops in price are too risky for a long term investment and too volatile for short term investments. As of July 2022, Bitcoin was down 72% from its all-time high. Cost of operations could potentially drive the price of cryptocurrencies down even more.

As the miners (computers, nodes) around the world use high powered computers for digital mining it is estimated that they use more than 86 terawatthours (TWh) of electricity per year, most of the mining is done in the United States. That is more electricity than the countries of Finland or Belgium use per year! (25) Suppose the government places higher fees on miners for their significant use of electricity? At a time when the world is dealing with global warming that is a possibility! What if miners decide that maintaining expensive equipment or paying higher utility bills is no longer supported by meager returns on their investments? After all, the reward for solving a blockchain goes only to one miner, so participation in creating blockchain solutions seems more like a gamble than a business activity that has predictable returns on investment!

My negative position on cryptocurrency might not be popular. After all, human psychology favors new, innovative things. It's like our interest in the new guy or girl who transfers to our school in the middle of the school year! Everyone wants to know their story! Who is this mysterious person? Maybe I should be the first to introduce myself? Maybe being with them will add to my popularity?

I encourage people to diversify their investments, but I don't recommend an investment solely because it *can be* profitable. What virtue does the investment have? What connection does your life have with it? What benefit is the product or service to humanity, the government, or business?

With so little known about crypto (other than its high volatility in price) the explanation for its popularity is primarily the potential for profit.

Two emotions that should not influence our investment decisions are fear and greed. Perhaps many fear being left behind, missing the boat with the brand new thing. Greed rears its ugly head when talk of unprecedented profits made the news in 2020. Perhaps if you did not buy crypto between 2013 and 2016 you have already missed the boat!

I recommend crypto only to those with a high risk tolerance. I recommend no more than 1 to 2% of one's investments be in crypto and only money they can afford to lose. To loosely quote Warren Buffett, invest in companies you like and know something about. All we seem to know about cryptocurrency is that it *can* make money. But some can also make money at the casino and the racetrack. Except I don't plan to use them for my retirement income.

CHAPTER 27
Afterword

I hope I have been able to help you with some concepts and strategies that will be profitable to you. Writing this book often brought to mind why I first became an accountant and a financial planner – to help others financially.

In the 1950s and 60s, my father worked as a handyman and my mother worked as a maid. Yet we seemed to have all we needed from one day to the next. But that experience taught me what it meant to be working-class. When you must use your labor to earn a living, you feel different about things than when money is earning money for you. Those whose labor provides their living and those whose money provides their living will often have different attitudes about politics, government, business, society, and even one another. My education in economics began when I was a very young man.

When I was in high school dressing well was very important. We wore hand-tailored pants and Italian knit shirts to school two or three times a week and dress shirts with ties at least one day a week. So at age 15 I needed work just to keep up with the fashions in school. My first job was work as a Bus Boy. By the time I joined the Air Force I had made mattresses, laid carpet, and worked as a Pile Driver. I have worked in both labor-intensive jobs and mentally challenging jobs, but I have always worked, attended school, or both.

Being a financial advisor should not be as difficult as it has been. Because of the great need for financial advice and its value, persons with financial knowledge should be paid fair wages that reflect their worth. But the financial services industry exposes clients to the risks of the marketplace while holding advisors in captive employment arrangements without the security of a regular salary. That needs to change.

In 2001, before studying to become a financial planner, I thought of leaving the world of finance altogether. Why worry about the financial conditions of others? The weight on my spirit made me think about going into a completely different line of work. Perhaps worry was the price one paid for seeing things in terms of money? The accounting profession enabled me to provide for my family and myself, but I didn't consider the cost of caring about the financial challenges of others. How much more of my spirit would be sacrificed if I continued to measure things in terms of income and expenses, or assets and liabilities?

I didn't consider back then that worry was a normal human emotion. In President Franklin Roosevelt's 1941 State of the Union Address, the third freedom he wished for Americans (and the world) was "freedom from want"! Even in my small station in life, I appreciated the cares of others and I worried that I didn't know enough to help them. I was at a crossroads. Should I learn more about the world of finance or just wipe my hands of finance altogether?

My decision was to learn financial planning. I thought if I could learn more about money instead of running away, perhaps I would find peace. But even after mastering the principles of finance that enabled me to help others, I didn't account for a financial services industry culture that has difficulty balancing money with professional, community, and societal needs.

Today, I am reminded of the forces that work against financial professionals having successful careers and the implications of those forces for the financial lives of most Americans. So the worry is still there in spite of my additional knowledge. I can only find solace in knowing I have been able to help a few.

I will close with an idea that I learned in business school that at the time seemed contrary to my values. At least one professor impressed upon us that if a business was to succeed it had to grow. If that was true about business, it may be true about our financial lives too. We need to grow in harmony with our values, our community, society, and the environment, but we need to grow.

When people of merit are financially secure, we will have better social order and the ability to withstand threats to the democratic process. We will be in a better position to survive divisive elected officials who lead others to destructive thoughts, ideas, *and behaviors.*

Whatever our instincts or attitudes toward the acquisition of power or material things, we need to come to grips with the economic system in which we find ourselves. *How* we grow and for what purpose is still up to us!

I don't mean we need to join the rat race or keep up with the Joneses. I mean we have to create a foundation with moral and financial principles that give us the power to rise above emotions like fear and greed that have been the downfall of so many. The combination of moral and financial integrity will give us the power we so dearly need to face the struggles a capitalistic society brings with it.

Our visions are as unique as our fingerprints. Use your vision and the principles of finance to shape a better world for yourself and others.

A long journey begins with the first step. I hope in some way I have helped you prepare for it. Along the way, may you experience peace, and witness beauty.

Bibliography

(1) Fox, Michelle. 2019. "99% of Americans Don't Use a Financial Advisor — Here's Why." CNBC. CNBC. November 11, 2019. https://www.cnbc.com/2019/11/11/99percent-of-americans-dont-use-a-financial-advisor-heres-why.html/

(2) Rosen, Miriam, and Financial IQ. 2020. "Merrill Reveals Breakdown of Minority FAs; Transparency Is 'Very Healthy.'" August 21, 2020. Merrill Reveals Breakdown of Minority FAs; Transparency is "Very Healthy". https://financialadvisoriq.com/c/2857123/351753?referrer_module=searchSubFromFAIQ&highlight=Merrill%20Reveals%20Breakdown%20of%20Minority%20FAs/

(3) Financial Advisor IQ, and Alex Padalka. 2020a. "Morgan Stanley to Pay $950K to Finra, Customers over Alleged Churning." Financial Advisor IQ. August 14, 2020. https://financialadvisoriq.com/c/2849413/349773/morgan_stanley_finra_customers_over_alleged_churning?referrer_module=emailMorningNews&module_order=15&login=1&code=ZDJkamNHRkFjUzVqYjIwc0lERXhOelF5TnpNekxDQXhNRFEyT0Rjd05UWT/

(4) FA Accused of Running Ponzi Scheme Charged with Murdering Client. Financial Advisor IQ. November 19, 2020. https://financialadvisoriq.com/c/2967413/363103/accused_running_ponzi_scheme_charged_with_murdering_client?referrer_module=emailMorningNews&module_order=15&login=1&code=ZDJkamNHRkFjUzVqYjIwc0lERXhOelF5TnpNekxDQXpNemN5TnpReE5EST0/

(5) Padalka, Alex. 2021. "Ex-Merrill FA Who Stole from Man Framed for Rape, Murder Heads to Prison." August 13, 2021. https://www. financialadvisoriq.com/c/3286464/415254/merrill_stole_from_framed_rape_murder_heads_prison?referrer_module=issue-Headline/

(6) Financial Advisor IQ, and Andrew Kessel Comments. 2021. "SEC Chair: Too Many Fraudsters, Ponzi Schemers, Cons Preying on Investors." Financial Advisor IQ. November 5, 2021. https://www. financialadvisoriq.com/c/3388254/430984/chair_many_fraudsters_ponzi_schemers_cons_preying_investors?referrer_module=issue-Headline&module_order=2/

(7) Robert Bernard Reich. 2015. *Saving Capitalism : For the Many, Not the Few.* London: Icon Books. (Page 10)

(8) Financial Advisor IQ, and 2021. 2021. "LPL Kicks out FA over Alleged 'Racist' Remarks Leaked on TikTok." Financial Advisor IQ. August 5, 2021. https://www.financialadvisoriq.com/c/3274914/413754/kicks_over_alleged_racist_remarks_leaked_tiktok?referrer_module=issueHeadline&module_order=5/.

(9) Rosen, Miriam. 2020. "Merrill, Edward Jones Lead in FA Trainees Numbers; Many Likely to Fail." August 11, 2020. https://financialadvisoriq.com/c/2843943/349743/merrill_edward_jones_lead_trainees_numbers_many_likely_fail?referrer_module=emailMorningNews&module_order=12&login=1&code=ZDJkamNHRkFjUz-VqYjIwc0lERXhOelF5TnpNekxDQXhPRE0yTlRnMk5EZ3c/

(10) President Ronald Reagan. https://www.reaganfoundation.org/ronald-reagan/reagan-quotes-speeches/news-conference-1/

(11) Fareed Zakaria. Fareed Zakaria, GPS. April 2021 https://edition.cnn.com/videos/tv/2021/04/04/exp-gps-0404-fareeds-take.cnn/

(12) Ibbotson, Morningstar, Debra Brede, and Bing.com/images. n.d. "Ibbotson Chart 1926-2019." Accessed December 6, 2021. https://debrabrede.com/wp-content/uploads/sites/43/2020/07/Stocks-Bond-Bills-Inflation-Ibbotson-2019_Page_1-1.jpg/.

(13) Statista. Wealth distribution in the United States in the first quarter of 2022 https://www.statista.com/statistics/203961/wealth-distribution-for-the-us/

(14) Sarah Naussauer. Sept 2, 2021. Walmart to Raise Minimum Wage to $12 an Hour. Wall Street Journal. https://www.wsj.com/articles/walmart-gives-raises-to-more-than-565-000-store-workers-11630607667?cx_testId=3&cx_testVariant=cx_2&cx_artPos=1&mod=WTRN#cxrecs_s/

(15) Friedberg, Barbara. 2019. "7 Best Socially Conscious Mutual Funds." Money.usnews.com. U.S. News & World Report. October 23, 2019. https://money.usnews.com/investing/funds/slideshows/best-socially-responsible-mutual-funds/

(16) Friedman, Zack. 2020. "Student Loan Debt Statistics in 2020: A Record $1.6 Trillion." Forbes. February 3, 2020. https://www.forbes.com/sites/zackfriedman/2020/02/03/student-loan-debt-statistics/#5b25a30c281f/.

(17) U.S Department of Health & Human Services. 2020. "2020 Poverty Guidelines." ASPE. January 21, 2020. https://aspe.hhs.gov/2020-poverty-guidelines/.

(18) U.S. Department of Education. 2000. "Home | U.S. Department of Education." Ed.gov. 2000. https://www.ed.gov/.

(19) Federal Student Aid U.S. Department of Education. 2020. "Federal Student Aid." Studentaid.gov. 2020. https://studentaid.gov/manage-loans/repayment/plans/income-driven/. 123

(20) Tax Policy Center. Brookings Institution. May 2020. https://www.taxpolicycenter.org/briefing-book/who-pays-estate-tax/

(21) Matt Hougan & David Lawant. "The Guide to Bitcoin, Blockchain, and Cryptocurrency for Investment Professionals." Bitwise, Advisor Whitepapers., January 8, 2021. https://bitwiseinvestments.com/crypto-market-insights/the-guide-to-bitcoin-blockchain-and-cryptocurrency-for-investment-professionals/

(22) Sephton, Conner. 2022 "How Many Cryptocurrencies are there?" January 27, 2022. https://currency.com/how-many-cryptocurrencies-are-there/

(23) Joseph R. Biden, Executive Order on Ensuring Responsible Development of Digital Assets https://www.federalregister.gov/documents/2022/03/14/2022-05471/ensuring-responsible-development-of-digital-assets/ March 9, 2022

(24) Cryptocurrency Prices by Market Cap https://www.coingecko.com/ July 14, 2022

(25) Cambridge Bitcoin Electricity Consumption Index https://ccaf.io/cbeci/index/comparisons/

Glossary

10-Percent Tax Penalty – The IRS levies a 10-percent penalty on early withdrawals from retirement accounts, deferred compensation, and certain permanent insurance accounts before age 59.5. This penalty is assessed on top of one's regular income tax. There are a limited number of exceptions to the penalty.

401k Plan – A defined *contribution* retirement plan set up by employers to provide retirement benefits to employees. Many employers provide a "match" of the amounts that an employee contributes to the plan up to a percentage of the employees' salary, often between 1 and 5 percent. There are usually time requirements before employer contributions are made (one to two years of employment). There may also be time requirements for "vesting" (when the employee has rights to the contributions made by the employer). Some plans allow employees to borrow against the balance in the account.

AARP – American Association of Retired Persons

Accumulation Phase – The time period in which a person contributes to a retirement account or life insurance policy (as opposed to the withdrawal phase as in retirement).

Actively Managed – A term describing mutual funds where a mutual fund manager determines which stocks or bonds to be included. The fund manager decides when to buy and sell the stocks and bonds. Index funds, on the other hand, have no managers.

Activities of Daily Living (ADL) – The activities considered in relation to long-term care policies (bathing, eating, getting out of bed, dressing, and toileting). When a policy holder cannot perform two or more of these activities, the long-term care policy is "triggered."

Adjusted Gross Income (AGI) – A reference to the last line of page one of the tax form 1040. The figure is often used to qualify for a mortgage or determine qualification for government benefits. It includes income from all sources reduced by certain allowable deductions. *Taxable Income* is determined by subtracting the standard or itemized deductions and personal exemptions from the adjusted gross income.

American Opportunity Credit – An education credit, the American Opportunity Tax Credit is available for the first four years of college.

Annuitant – The person expected to receive the payouts from an annuity.

Balanced Funds – Mutual funds that include both stocks and bonds.

Blue Book, Kelly–Fair Market Range and other pricing details to give you a real look at what a car should cost in your area. The Kelley Blue Book® Price Advisor is a range-based pricing tool to help car buyers and sellers talk about price.

Bonds – A debt instrument issued by the government or a corporation to borrow money from an investor. Bonds are safer than stock or real estate investments because their value fluctuates less. Interest is paid to investors based on the coupon rate associated with the bond. Government bonds usually pay less interest than corporate bonds since they have beneficial tax features and are safer.

Brokerage Account – An investment account that is not a retirement account (IRA, 401K, etc.). Earnings on brokerage accounts are taxed annually. Earnings are not deferred until they are withdrawn as with retirement or deferred compensation accounts. Though earnings are currently taxed, capital gains and qualified dividends are taxed at a long-term capital gains tax rate if the investment is held more than one year.

Capital Gains – The difference between the cost of an investment and the amount it was sold for. Long-term capital gains occur if an investment is held one year or more (LTCG). If held one year or less, the gain would be short-term. LTCG are taxed at a lower rate than salaries and other income. Short-term capital gains are taxed at the same rate as salaries and other income (the "ordinary" tax rate). See the chapter on taxes for the different LTCG rates.

Certificates of Deposit – Short-term paper investments issued by banks. They can be for periods of three, six, nine, or twelve months. The longer the period, the higher the interest rate paid. The interest rates are generally higher than a savings account but less than the coupon rates for bonds. They may be insured by the FDIC (Federal Deposit Insurance Corporation).

Churning – Describes a financial advisor's unethical behavior of executing unnecessary trades to earn a commission (i.e., needless buying and selling of similar mutual funds).

Commission – A fee charged as a percentage of an amount invested. Average commissions can run 5 percent of the purchase transaction. The higher the percentage, the less principal remains to be invested.

Cryptocurrency–A digital asset, a medium of exchange that relies on cryptography (i.e., blockchain).

Defined Benefit Plan – A pension benefit provided by employers for the life of the retiree. A life annuity usually based on years of service and pay grade at time of retirement. Few remain today except for government employees.

Diversify – A modern term meaning don't put all your eggs in one basket. A well-diversified portfolio will include a broad range of investments (stocks, bonds, REITS, International, index, or managed funds).

Implied Interest – The financial cost for the use of money but not expressed in a contract.

Index Fund – A mutual fund that is not managed (i.e., the Fortune 500 Index fund). Owners of these funds are compensated based on the performance of the stocks included in the index.

Managed Funds – Mutual funds that are managed by investment managers. Investment managers choose which stocks (or bonds) to buy and include in the mutual fund. The fund manager also makes decisions about selling. Many fund managers may be restricted by fund style (large cap, small cap, growth, etc.).

Mortality and Expense – Fees charged by an insurance company to cover their payouts for life insurance and other expenses.

Mutual Fund – An investment that includes a number of different stocks or bonds. The fund may have as few as thirty stocks or bonds or thousands in some cases. Mutual funds may be managed or index.

Nest Egg – An informal term used to describe the estimated amount of money needed (or desired) to retire comfortably.

No Load – A broker/dealer who sells investments without charging the purchaser a commission. Different mutual funds with the broker/dealer or mutual fund company may have management fees, but they are generally less than 1 percent. Most of these fees will be less than half of 1 percent—.005, .0025 in the case of Index funds.

Payable on Death (POD) – The term used to describe the disposition of an investment upon the death of the investor. The beneficiary listed on a POD contract will be in a superior position to claims of others.

Portfolio – This generally describes the inventory of investments held by an individual. The portfolio may consist of mutual funds and individual stocks or bonds. A well-diversified portfolio will include a broad range of investments. A good portfolio will also have a good balance of stocks versus bonds, inclusive of more bond funds as the investor ages.

Premature Distribution – The act of taking money out of a retirement plan, deferred compensation plan, insurance contract, or annuity before one reaches age 59.5. This usually results in a tax penalty of 10 percent of the amount withdrawn. See the section on taxes for possible exceptions to the penalty.

Pre-Tax Items – Transactions that reduce one's W-2 taxable wage amount or other "above the line" transactions that reduce adjusted gross income. Examples include cafeteria plan items and contributions to 401Ks and deferred compensation plans. The deduction for a Traditional IRA has the same impact.

Principal – The balance of an investment or debt (as opposed to principle—a rule or guide).

Probate – In general, the process by which the state passes the legal title of property to a deceased person's heirs. The process may take more than one year to complete.

Real Estate Investment Trust (REIT) – A mutual fund that includes stocks of real estate companies. Some REITs may focus on commercial properties, and some focus on residential properties. REITs are required to pay out 90 percent of their profits to investors each year.

Rate of Return – A term used to gauge how profitable an investment has been or has the potential to be. It's often expressed as a percentage (i.e., 10 percent). It can be a combination of capital gains and interests and dividends received on the investment. To obtain it, you would add these three components of profit together and divide the result by the original investment amount.

Rebalance – A term used to describe bringing the current ratio of stocks versus bonds in a portfolio in line with the historic or desired ratio of stocks to bonds (or stock funds or bond funds). In the ordinary course of business, stocks will outperform bonds. So if the desired and beginning ratio of stocks to bonds was 60 percent stocks and 40 percent bonds, after a time because of the growth of stocks, that ratio could have become 70 percent stocks to 30 percent bonds. So if an investor still wanted a 60:40-percent ratio, he or she would need to sell some stocks and buy some bonds.

Required Minimum Distribution (RMD) – The minimum amount to be taken out annually from investments once an investor turns age seventy-two. The requirement does not apply to Roth IRAs or brokerage accounts. (Congress was attempting to raise the age to 75 beginning in 2022). See chapter on retirement.

Revenue Sharing – The distribution of a portion of federal tax revenues to state and local governments.

Risk Tolerance – A subjective mindset or objective financial condition that describes an investor's ability to handle the risk involved in the movement of the stock or bond market. Subjective describes the individual's mood or attitude. Objective describes the individual's financial ability to weather the ups and downs of the market. Advisors like to determine an investor's risk tolerance (on a scale of one to ten) before recommending investments.

Roth IRA – An IRA that does not currently provide a tax deduction. Its benefit is that if left for at least five years and one has reached age 59.5, all earnings could be received tax-free. There is also no requirement to redeem any of the investment (no RMD) beginning at age seventy-two. See chapter on retirement.

Standard Deduction – The deduction the IRS provides to each taxpayer or couple based upon their filing status—Married filing jointly, Head of household, Single, or Married filing separately. The amount is subtracted from your adjusted gross income similar to an exemption. If one has significant mortgage interest expense, property taxes, charitable contributions, and *enormous* medical expenses, they may have higher *Itemized Deductions* and thus choose to itemize instead of taking the standard deduction.

Target Date – A description used for life-cycle mutual funds. The target date is the date the mutual fund matures. These funds are designed to rebalance yearly to provide an ideal ratio of stocks to bonds as one approaches the target date. The further out the target date, the more aggressive the fund is currently. By the time the target date arrives, one is assumed to be retired, and thus the fund will consist of mostly bonds. See further discussion in the chapter on investing.

Tax Deferred – Describes the practice of postponing the tax on earnings until those earnings are withdrawn. Taxes can be deferred on earnings in retirement accounts, annuities, and permanent life insurance policies. Taxes are not deferred on brokerage accounts; they are taxed currently.

Tax Evasion – Ignoring one's responsibility for taxes on income or earnings.

Taxable Income – An amount determined after deductions and personal exemptions have been subtracted from the adjusted gross income. Dividing this number by your calculated taxes will let you know your *effective* tax rate. These amounts are determined before any tax credits or additional taxes.

Teacher Loan Forgiveness Program – A program whereby some student loan debt is forgiven for teaching in low-income school districts. See chapter on student loans.

Time Horizon – Generally describes the time period an investment will be held. An important concept because the shorter the time horizon (less than five years), the more risk involved in choosing an investment—especially stocks. It could also describe the time period that distributions from the investment are expected to last.

Traditional IRA – IRAs that allow the amount contributed to them to be deducted from your gross income. See the chapter on retirement.

CPSIA information can be obtained
at www.ICGtesting.com
Printed in the USA
BVHW072305240123
657000BV00003B/18